ARROYO CENTER

STRATEGIC EXPOSURE

PROLIFERATION AROUND THE MEDITERRANEAN

IAN O. LESSER ◆ ASHLEY J. TELLIS

PREPARED FOR THE UNITED STATES ARMY

APPROVED FOR PUBLIC RELEASE; DISTRIBUTION UNLIMITED

RAND

The proliferation of weapons of mass destruction—nuclear, chemical and biological—and the means for their delivery at ever longer ranges has emerged as a leading issue in the post–Cold War debate about international security and as a prominent concern of U.S. policymakers and Army planners. Nowhere are the effects of proliferation trends felt more keenly than around the Mediterranean, where the European and Middle Eastern security environments meet, and where NATO allies are increasingly exposed to the spillover effects of instability to the south.

Our analysis explores proliferation trends in North Africa and the Levant (the Eastern Mediterranean and its hinterlands), the motives of proliferators around the region, and the implications for European security and for U.S., NATO, and Army policy.

This report summarizes research on "Weapons of Mass Destruction in North Africa and the Levant: The Search for Strategic Weight and the Political-Military Implications for the United States," a project sponsored by the Deputy Chief of Staff for Intelligence, U.S. Army, and conducted in the Arroyo Center's Strategy and Doctrine Program. The Arroyo Center is a federally funded research and development center sponsored by the United States Army.

CONTENTS

TABLES

A leading post–Cold War security interest of U.S. policymakers and strategists is the proliferation of nuclear, chemical, and biological weapons of mass destruction (WMDs) and the means for their delivery at ever longer ranges. For the military services, including the U.S. Army, proliferation trends and their regional effects are matters of great operational and strategic significance, with serious implications for U.S. freedom of action in future crises. Nowhere is the prospect of the spread of WMDs likely to have a more pronounced effect on strategic perceptions than around the Mediterranean. We analyzed proliferation trends and regional security consequences in the Mediterranean region and reached the following conclusions.

STATUS AND TRENDS

Many of the world's leading WMD proliferators are arrayed along Europe's southern periphery, and WMD risks are transforming the security environment in the Mediterranean as well as in Europe's regions. Key states south and east of the Mediterranean either possess or are in the process of acquiring WMDs, along with the means for delivering them across the Mediterranean. Iran already has a substantial chemical-weapons capability and is pursuing nuclear and biological capabilities. It has an active long-range ballistic missile development program and has moved toward acquiring significant numbers of deep-strike aircraft (a WMD delivery system that is often overlooked). Iraq's weapon programs are on hold while UN sanctions prevail, but Baghdad is in a position to develop chemical and biological weapons quickly once those sanctions are lifted. Egypt also has active chemical-weapons and long-range missile development programs.

Both Libya and Syria have chemical weapons (Libya also has a biological capability), and Algeria has been pushing ahead with development of a nuclear infrastructure. Like Iran, Iraq, and Egypt, all three countries have received help in developing or acquiring both WMDs and delivery systems from external sources such as China and North Korea. Unlike Iran, Iraq, and Egypt, the countries farther to the west do not yet have the indigenous industrial base needed to pursue such weapon systems on their own. They are thus more dependent on their supplier network, but the risks posed by Libya and Syria (and potentially Algeria) are nonetheless real for at least as long as that network lasts.

Within ten years, it is possible that every southern European capital will be within range of ballistic missiles based in North Africa or the Levant. Turkish population centers are already exposed to missiles based in Syria and Iran (and Iraq). Southern European, French, and Turkish security debates and policies are being influenced to a considerable degree by the perception of risks emanating from the south (in the Turkish case, from the Middle East), above all proliferation risks. In some instances, perceptions have outstripped the reality of system ranges and capabilities. But proliferation trends suggest that European concerns may soon be justified.

Political turmoil in North Africa and the greater Middle East reinforces proliferation risks in the Mediterranean. The potential advent of a radical Islamic regime in Algeria, with its nuclear ambitions and missile interests, could accelerate proliferation trends across North Africa and worsen the outlook for WMD threats in times of crisis. Violent political change in North Africa could encourage broader WMD-based alliances in the Middle East (Algeria-Syria-Iran, for instance), compounding the proliferation challenge.

WMD proliferation in North Africa and the Levant will continue to be fueled by systemic, regional, and internal motives. Key regional actors, including Algeria, Libya, Egypt, Syria, and Iran, are engaged in an active search for geopolitical "weight" and national prestige in the post–Cold War world. Even modest WMD capabilities or the mere pursuit of such capabilities are seen as contributing to these states' ability to be taken seriously in Muslim, Arab, and "Southern" circles, and on the international scene as a whole. At the same time, regional frictions and multiple internal and external challenges provide motives for proliferation.

The spread of WMD and longer-range delivery systems suggests that traditional distinctions between European and Middle Eastern security are eroding. Europe is increasingly exposed to the retaliatory consequences of Western—especially U.S.—action beyond Europe. Hints of this development could be seen in the Persian Gulf experience, when the popular reaction in North Africa and the potential for terrorist attacks on European soil were matters of concern, especially to southern Europeans. In future crises of this nature, the proliferation of WMD and longer-range delivery systems will create the potential for brinkmanship, either by affected states in the Middle East or their allies in North Africa. In effect, the spread of long-range weapons enables possessor states at some remove from centers of conflict to play a role in events far from their own borders.

For the moment, however, the most pressing WMD risks are South-South, and the neighbors of proliferators in North Africa and the Levant are the most likely first victims of WMD use. The North-South dimensions of WMD proliferation could become more prominent with the spread of longer-range delivery systems and, as important, to the extent that political-military relations across the Mediterranean worsen.

IMPLICATIONS FOR POLICY AND STRATEGY

The presence of WMD will substantially complicate decisions regarding intervention beyond Europe, along with choices relating to the equipment, training, doctrine, and objectives of intervention forces. The preference for multinational operations in areas such as the Gulf and North Africa will add to this complexity, with potentially competing stakes, levels of WMD vulnerability, and capacity and tolerance for operations in a WMD environment.

Above all, the growing perception and reality of European exposure to WMD risks will affect the climate for cooperation in extra-European contingencies. The vulnerability of European population centers, especially in the context of ballistic missile threats, is likely to change

the calculus of cooperation in ways that will directly affect U.S. freedom of action and the capacity for power projection. Access to bases
and air space along the logistically vital Mediterranean–Indian
Ocean axis will be far less predictable under these conditions. Vulnerable allies may be reluctant to commit forces or even to support
U.S. action under some conditions. At a minimum, European cooperation—especially southern European and Turkish cooperation—
will come at a higher political and operational price.

*Specifically, countries exposed to WMD will demand greater reassur-
ance and deterrence against these risks.* This will take the form of requests for development and deployment of more capable antimissile
defenses, including the preemptive deployment of Patriot-like systems in times of crisis. More active treatment of WMD issues and
counterproliferation policy within NATO will almost certainly
emerge as a *sine qua non* for greater Alliance out-of-area involvement. In the absence of new antimissile and counterproliferation
initiatives, the prospects for unfettered access and cooperation in
future Gulf-like contingencies may well decline.

*Consideration should be given to specific technical and political-
strategic initiatives aimed at bolstering the security of Europe (and
U.S. forces operating around the Mediterranean) in the face of WMD
risks.* On the technical side, alternatives for mobile, rapidly deployable antimissile defenses in the Mediterranean deserve active exploration. To influence the calculus of cooperation in crises, such
systems should be able to go beyond merely symbolic defense of
population centers. The United States, in cooperation with key allies—not least France—should lead a reappraisal of Alliance strategy
regarding WMD threats from the Middle East. Responsiveness on
this issue may be just as vital to European security and the future of
NATO as the successful management of more familiar challenges in
the East.

*The prospect of continuing WMD proliferation around the Mediter-
ranean suggests a new class of contingencies, in which force may be
required for purposes of dissuasion, preemption, or retaliation in relation to WMD.* These missions will undoubtedly pose daunting challenges for strategic and tactical intelligence and precision strike of
mobile or hardened targets. In the case of unconventional delivery
systems, perhaps under the control of substate actors, additional

challenges would arise. Moreover, all of these factors will come into play in a multilateral context, with complex issues of political consensus, intelligence sharing, command and control, etc. More positively, it should be noted that the Mediterranean continues to be an area of extensive and regular military cooperation among the NATO allies, including those members outside the Alliance's integrated command structure (France and Spain), and that much useful infrastructure as well as a habit of cooperation already exist in the region.

ACKNOWLEDGMENTS

The research presented here benefited greatly from extensive discussions with official and unofficial observers in the United States and abroad. The authors wish to thank all those who contributed their views and expertise. We are particularly grateful to RAND colleagues James Quinlivan, Tom McNaugher, Jerrold Green, Bruce Hoffman, Mary Morris, Dean Wilkening, James Chiesa, and Graham Fuller, as well as Patrick Neary and Eric Kraemer of the Army Staff and Dr. Lisa Anderson of Columbia University, for their comments and assistance in carrying forward this research. Needless to say, any errors or omissions are the responsibility of the authors.

ABBREVIATIONS

AAM   Air-to-air missile

ACDA   (U.S.) Arms Control and Disarmament Agency

ACRS   Arms Control and Regional Security

APHE   Armor piercing high explosive

ASM   Air-to-surface missile

ASUW   Antisurface warfare

ASW   Antisubmarine warfare

ATBM   Antitactical ballistic missile

BAI   Battlefield air interdiction

CAS   Close air support

CEP   Circular error probable

COIN   Counterinsurgency

EU   European Union

FGA   Fighter–ground attack

GA   Ground attack

HE   High explosive

HEAT	High explosive antitank
HESH	High explosive squash head
IAEA	International Atomic Energy Agency
ICM	Improved conventional munitions
IR	Infrared
MLRS	Multiple launch rocket system
MRL	Multiple rocket launcher
MW	Megawatt
MWe	Megawatt electric
MWt	Megawatt thermal
NBC	Nuclear, biological, chemical (weapons)
NPT	Non-Proliferation Treaty
R&D	Research and development
RAP	Rocket-assisted projectile
SAM	Surface-to-air missile
SP	Self-propelled
SSM	Surface-to-surface missile
SubSM	Submarine-to-surface missile
WEU	Western European Union
WMD	Weapons of mass destruction

Chapter One

INTRODUCTION

The proliferation of weapons of mass destruction, including the means for their delivery at longer ranges, has emerged as a leading issue on the post–Cold War security agenda, and counterproliferation policy is an increasingly prominent interest of U.S. policymakers and strategists.[1] For the military services, including the U.S. Army, proliferation trends and their regional effects are matters of great operational and strategic significance, with serious implications for U.S. freedom of action in future crises. The experience of the Gulf War, including the discovery of a substantial Iraqi nuclear program, the threat of chemical and biological weapons, and the use of Scud missiles, brought proliferation issues to the forefront of public as well as expert attention. The lessons of the Gulf War with regard to weapons of mass destruction, especially their effect on perceptions and strategy, have also been of great interest to regional actors in the Middle East and elsewhere.

Nowhere has the prospect of the spread of weapons of mass destruction (WMD) had a more pronounced effect on strategic perceptions than around the Mediterranean. NATO's southern allies—Portugal, Spain, Italy, Greece and Turkey—as well as France, are especially vulnerable to the political and military consequences of instability across the Mediterranean and the Middle East as a whole. Vague fears (not so vague in the case of Turkey) of vulnerability to ballistic missile and air attack during the Gulf crisis have given rise to more

---

[1]For the purposes of this analysis, "weapons of mass destruction" are defined as nuclear, chemical, biological, and radiological arms, and the means for their delivery, including but not limited to ballistic missiles.

concrete concerns with the spread of more capable ballistic missile systems in Asia and the Middle East. With some notable exceptions, the perception of vulnerability to WMD in Europe outstrips the reality of WMD "reach" on Europe's southern periphery. But the longer-term trend is undoubtedly toward increasing European and Turkish exposure to systems based in North Africa and the Levant, and more broadly, to the retaliatory consequences of Western action in the greater Middle East.[2]

North Korea aside, the world's most active proliferators are arrayed along an arc stretching from Algeria to Pakistan. As a prominent French observer has noted, "A proper regard for security cannot exclude the hypothesis that several European cities will be—probably sooner than generally expected—the potential targets of these weapons."[3] Indeed, with the development and spread of ballistic missile systems on the pattern of North Korea's Nodong series, with ranges of 1,000 km or more, it is quite likely that by the turn of the century every European capital could be reached by missiles based in North Africa and the Levant.

From the perspective of U.S. strategy and planning, the growing exposure of NATO Europe to proliferation risks emanating from the south has considerable political-military and operational significance.

First, it suggests that traditional distinctions between European and Middle Eastern security are fading, with greater interdependence between developments in each region. The U.S. ability to project forces beyond Europe to southwest Asia and the Persian Gulf will continue to depend (as it did in the Gulf War) on access to bases and airspace in southern Europe. As the southern European allies of the United States become more vulnerable to retaliation, the European debate about cooperation in extra-European contingencies will become more complex and uncertain. At a minimum, the political and military "price" of this sort of security cooperation is bound to increase. If one adds to this equation the likelihood that the United

---

[2]"Levant" refers broadly to the eastern Mediterranean and its hinterlands. For the purposes of this report, the countries of interest in the Levant (and somewhat beyond) are Syria, Iraq, and Iran.

[3]Pierre Lellouche, "France in Search of Security," *Foreign Affairs*, Spring 1993, p. 124.

States will wish to see an ever greater European capacity for participation in defense of Gulf interests, the question of reassurance and deterrence against WMD risks takes on new importance.

Second, the strategic environment on Europe's periphery is characterized by numerous actual and potential flash points for conflict and crises that may demand a Western response. A full survey of potential contingencies along Europe's southern "arc of crisis" is beyond the scope of this report.[4] A far from exhaustive list would include: Moroccan action against the Spanish enclaves of Ceuta and Melilla across from Gibraltar; conflict between Morocco and Algeria, Libya and Tunisia, or Libya and Egypt; an Islamist revolution in Algeria and/or Egypt in which Western lives and interests are directly threatened; Western responses to terrorism sponsored by states in North Africa or the Levant; Iranian or Iraqi aggression in the Gulf; and Syrian, Iraqi, or Iranian conflict with Turkey. In each case, the operational and political climate for intervention would be influenced to a considerable extent by the potential for regional actors to bring WMD to bear. The ability to project and concentrate forces, the choice of objectives, and the duration of ground operations, if any, will all be affected.

Third, the character of military capabilities, including WMD, on Europe's periphery will be a key strategic issue in the overall evolution of relations between Muslim and Arab states and the West. These states, in common with other regional actors in the Third World, will look to increase their leverage in dealing with the West, and will seek to replace the advantages of Cold War patronage and nonalignment with new forms of geopolitical weight. The acquisition of WMD has emerged as an important dimension of this search for weight and prestige, regionally and on the wider international scene. The strategic relationship across the Mediterranean will be a critical theater for dialogue and conflict on WMD risks, demanding new applications of traditional concepts like stability and deterrence relevant along North-South lines.

---

[4]For a detailed treatment of Mediterranean security problems, see Ian O. Lesser, *Mediterranean Security: New Perspectives and Implications for U.S. Policy,* Santa Monica, CA: RAND, R-4178-AF, 1992; and Ian O. Lesser, *Security in North Africa: Internal and External Challenges,* Santa Monica, CA: RAND, MR-203-AF, 1993.

Chapter Two of this report explores the range of motives for acquiring WMD, the consequences of "virtual" versus actual proliferation, and the implications for regional stability.

Chapter Three addresses the strategic implications of the spread of WMD around the Mediterranean for European security, as well as more specific implications for military operations. Chapter Four summarizes our conclusions and offers implications for policy and strategy.

In the appendix we present the supporting data for our analysis. It surveys WMD capabilities and trends in selected countries of North Africa and the Levant, and it supplies substantial detail on delivery systems—from artillery to aircraft and ballistic missiles. We also assess capacity for indigenous development of WMD systems, together with the prospects for further development and purchases.

The data appearing in the appendix were drawn entirely from open sources, and no effort has been made to reconcile this information with data from classified holdings. The purpose of the appendix is not to provide a precise quantitative assessment of the risks emanating from North Africa and the Levant, but rather to suggest patterns with strategic implications and worthy of attention. Given this objective, unclassified literature is more than adequate to characterize the proliferation trends facing Europe and NATO in the south. Most important, the authors and the study sponsors believe that an unclassified treatment of the issue is essential to stimulate broader debate in the United States and abroad.

Chapter Two

MOTIVES FOR ACQUIRING WEAPONS OF MASS DESTRUCTION

An assessment of the extent and character of proliferation trends around the Mediterranean basin in the years ahead, as well as the most likely circumstances for the use of WMD, will benefit from a clearer understanding of the motives for acquiring mass destruction capabilities. Thinking through the problem of motives in a setting as varied as the Mediterranean basin is not an easy task. The countries featured in this analysis face a wide variety of internal and external challenges, giving rise to rather different proliferation dynamics. Nonetheless, a good deal can be observed or inferred from the actions and attitudes of regional states.

The question of motives for acquiring WMD can be explored at three levels. First, what are the systemic factors driving proliferation around the Mediterranean after the Cold War? Second, how do narrower, regional ambitions and concerns affect the desire for WMD? Finally, how may the internal situation in key states stimulate, support, or limit the pursuit of WMD capabilities?[1]

THE SEARCH FOR STRATEGIC WEIGHT

The leading proliferators around the Mediterranean have all been profoundly affected by the end of the Cold War, most in ways that

---

[1]A recent RAND study of decisionmaking and the motivations for proliferation addresses the security-related, organizational, and psychological aspects of this issue. See John Arquilla and Paul K. Davis, *Modeling Decisionmaking of Potential Proliferators as Part of Developing Counterproliferation Strategies,* Santa Monica, CA: RAND, MR-467, 1994.

have contributed to their insecurity. Libya, Syria, and Iraq saw their client-patron relationship with the Soviet Union weaken and finally dissolve as Moscow found itself unwilling and unable to provide the political and material backing of the Cold War years. The disintegration of the Soviet Union has virtually eliminated Moscow as a player in Middle Eastern affairs, except as a supplier of ex–Warsaw Pact equipment on a strictly commercial basis. The Russian security guarantee to its clients in the region, evident since Khrushchev's nuclear threats during the Suez crisis, has disappeared, leaving countries such as Libya, Syria, Iraq, and Algeria without any form of external, extended deterrence. Regional actors now must rely on indigenous political and military power. Indeed, the Soviet connection in the Middle East, while contributing to the weight of conventional and unconventional armament, also had a stabilizing influence. The risk of superpower escalation made Moscow (as well as Washington) extraordinarily sensitive to the dangers of regional conflict in places where Western intervention could not be ruled out. Thus, many would argue that the Iraqi invasion of Kuwait would not have been possible in the days when Baghdad depended on close ties to Moscow; the Soviets simply would not have allowed Saddam to attack Kuwait, for fear of the escalatory risks.

Even in the case of postrevolutionary Iran, the clear importance of Tehran's strategic orientation to both superpowers meant that the Iranian regime could benefit from a nonaligned position, playing superpower interests off against each other. The most striking example of nonalignment as an outlet for international activism and prestige could be seen in Algeria. Indeed, for Algiers, leadership in the nonaligned movement was the principal thrust of its foreign and security policy since the French withdrawal (in reality, Algerian military policy was heavily dependent on ties to the Soviet Union and Eastern Europe). Thus nonalignment as well as alignment served as potent sources of strategic "weight" for countries across the Middle East and North Africa. In the post–Cold War world, these countries have lost these moorings for foreign and security policy, and most are now engaged in an active search for new sources of geostrategic weight, some benign (e.g., half-hearted attempts at regional integration), others less so.[2] The pursuit of WMD development has emerged as a leading vehicle for prestige, assertiveness, and attention in the post–Cold War world.

The Algerian leadership, for example, is keenly aware of the effect that its enigmatic nuclear program has on Western opinion, especially in the wake of allegations that Algeria might have been the recipient of nuclear materials smuggled out of Iraq during the Gulf crisis.[3] In the words of one Algerian, a leading analyst and former high-ranking diplomat, "In ten years time there will be two countries in Africa which are taken seriously by the United States—South Africa and Algeria—both will be nuclear powers."[4] The statement was not necessarily meant as a reference to nuclear weapons, although this cannot be ruled out. Most likely, it was intended to highlight the significance of civilian nuclear power programs for international prestige and the capacity of states in peripheral locations to be "taken seriously" by the West. Even fleeting evidence of the ability and interest in acquiring WMD capabilities draws Western attention.

The very fact that a state in North Africa or the Levant is pursuing or *might* pursue WMD capabilities provides a basis for diplomatic blackmail of a subtle kind, even in cases where the potential proliferator has extensive ties with the West. The primacy of proliferation concerns in the Western strategic debate provides considerable scope for states to signal, implicitly or explicitly: "Pay due attention to our regional security concerns/development requirements/desire for strategic reassurance, etc., or else." Put another way, "How much will you pay me *not* to go nuclear"?

---

[2]The Arab Union of the Maghreb, embracing Mauritania, Morocco, Algeria, Tunisia, and Libya, is aimed at promoting economic integration and political cooperation. More importantly, it represented, in theory, a vehicle for defusing regional tensions (e.g., between Morocco and Algeria over the Western Sahara) and giving the Maghreb countries greater weight in dealing with the West, especially the European Union. It has been largely unsuccessful on all counts.

[3]See, among other sources, "Saddam Helps Algeria Make Islamic Nuclear Bomb," *Sunday Times* (London), January 5, 1992; "Algeria and the Bomb," *The Economist,* January 11, 1992; and Youssef Ibrahim, "Algeria Offers Atom Arms Vow," *The New York Times,* January 8, 1992.

[4]Author's interview (Lesser), Algiers, May 1993.

At the international level, transfers of WMD systems and technologies, including cooperative development programs, may also serve to cement strategic alliances across regions and, to use a much-contested term, "civilizations." The latter possibility is highlighted by Samuel Huntington in his "clash of civilizations" paradigm, pointing to the growing ties between leading proliferators in the Muslim world (Syria, Iran, Libya, Algeria) and suppliers of nuclear and ballistic missile technology in East Asia.[5] Whether these connections are based on shared strategic interests that may or may not be enduring (for example, confrontation with the West) or simply commercial convenience is far from clear. But transfers of WMD systems and technology do have the potential of serving broader patterns of conflict and cooperation. WMD capabilities have already become a central issue in the strategic relationship between key Muslim states and the West. To the extent that relations between Islam and the West deteriorate across the board and begin to acquire the hallmarks of a wider, "civilizational" clash, the notion of an "Islamic bomb" (as well as less sophisticated forms of WMD and the means for their delivery) could have significance beyond the competition with Israel.

The United States should be concerned—as a matter of prudence— about the possibility of cascading proliferation of WMD across the entire region, from Algeria to Pakistan. Such a development would no doubt represent the worst case but must nonetheless be considered coercive diplomacy, since it could influence the prospects for brinkmanship in international crises. As an example, a new crisis in the Gulf followed by Western intervention, with widespread support for Iraq in a North Africa armed with nuclear and/or ballistic missiles could pose risks for southern Europe as well as U.S. forces in the Mediterranean. In short, a broadly based pattern of cooperative, coercive diplomacy involving WMD, however fragile over the long term, could seriously complicate European and American political choices in a crisis. Active proliferators such as Iran and Libya may find WMD an increasingly attractive means of building international "alliances," even if these are only transient arrangements with respect to certain narrow issue areas. They may also find it a convenient means of extending their political "reach" until they acquire weapons and delivery systems of true transregional range. Ultimately, WMD brink-

---

[5]See Samuel Huntington, "The Clash of Civilizations?" *Foreign Affairs*, Summer 1993.

manship by a sympathetic state across the Mediterranean on behalf of allies as far away as southeast Asia would be highly incredible. But Western planners could not ignore entirely the diplomatic and political complications accompanying such possibilities.

In a more benign sense, regional actors around the southern and eastern Mediterranean will see their WMD-related programs as contributing to the general level of Arab, Muslim, or Third World technological development. Civilian nuclear power projects and dual-use chemical and aerospace projects provide ample opportunity for building international prestige in a post–Cold War setting.[6]

REGIONAL MOTIVES

The character of the post–Cold War international system provides powerful longer-term motives for acquiring or exploring the acquisition of WMD. But more proximate, regional motives will almost certainly continue to be leading factors in the proliferation dynamic, often reinforcing or outweighing systemic motives. Motives flowing from regional security concerns will vary considerably from state to state, but a few generalizations are in order. First, looking at the Mediterranean region as a whole, the states to the south all face serious internal and external challenges: they are profoundly insecure and, in some instances, highly militarized societies. Under these conditions, the acquisition of WMD capabilities will have special advantages and risks. Second, as one moves eastward around the Mediterranean, the external, interstate challenges take on a more dramatic military flavor, with WMD capabilities more clearly linked to military balances and strategic competition. The regional competition between Morocco and Algeria or Libya and Egypt, while serious, cannot be compared with the Iraqi-Iranian confrontation or with the potential magnitude of friction among Turkey, Iran, and Russia in the Caucasus. Third, the confrontation with Israel has been

---

[6]For a useful survey of nuclear programs and ties in the Middle East, see Leonard S. Spector and Nancy Blabey, "Nuclear Proliferation Threats in the Islamic Middle East," *New Outlook*, September–October 1991; and Robert D. Blackwill and Albert Carnesale (eds.), *New Nuclear Nations: Consequences for U.S. Policy*, New York: Council on Foreign Relations, 1993.

a central element in the rhetoric of states in North Africa and the Levant with regard to WMD programs.

What are the implications of an environment in which the salience of the Arab-Israeli confrontation is declining? Recent frictions over Israel's undeclared nuclear arsenal in the Non-Proliferation Treaty (NPT) review conference, and the chilling effect of this issue on negotiations in the multilateral Arms Control and Regional Security (ACRS) talks, suggest that in the near term the Arab-Israeli competition is likely to remain a centerpiece of regional perceptions in the WMD arena. Over the longer term, progress on the bilateral track of the Middle East peace process is likely to reveal a more complex, diverse pattern of proliferation motives and concerns (e.g., Iran/Iraq, Egypt/Libya, Algeria/Morocco, Syria/Turkey).

Regional Factors in the Western Mediterranean

Morocco has not sought to purchase or develop WMD capabilities, although it regards Algeria as a serious regional competitor with a history of confrontation and conflict over border issues and the insurgency in the Western Sahara. With the deepening political crisis in Algeria and the possibility that a new Islamic regime may come to power in Algiers, Rabat may eventually confront a more active Islamist or nationalist challenge from Algeria. Under these conditions, Algeria's nuclear and ballistic missile ambitions may emerge as a more proximate threat to Morocco. Pursuit of a nuclear deterrent is almost certainly out of the question, but Rabat could well seek to build its air and missile capabilities in response. These would also be useful in the context of friction with Spain over control of the Spanish enclaves of Ceuta and Melilla on the Moroccan coast.[7]

Algeria's nuclear and ballistic missile programs are useful vehicles for asserting its regional weight, especially in relation to bilateral frictions with Morocco, whose ties with Europe and the United States are more highly developed. With its resources, population, history

---

[7]The defense of the enclaves is a leading concern of Spanish defense planners. The difficulty of defending the enclaves without creating a substantial defensive perimeter on Moroccan territory suggests to some Spanish analysts the necessity for a strategy of horizontal escalation, striking at targets of value elsewhere in Morocco proper. A more potent Moroccan retaliatory capability would complicate this approach.

(Algerians view their revolution as on a par with those of Russia and China), and tradition of international activism, Algeria regards itself as the dominant power in the Maghreb and a leading player in Arab, Muslim, and Third World politics. This suggests that despite the country's current political crisis (near–civil war), Algeria's desire for regional preeminence will eventually reassert itself—quite possibly in the service of an Islamist rather than nationalist regime. In this context, Algeria's regional motives for pursuing WMD are likely to expand. Indeed, the longer and more violent the Islamist struggle in Algeria, the greater the risk of a truly radical regime coming to power. Such a regime might seek to accelerate and give a distinctly anti-Western flavor to WMD programs.

In terms of international involvement and attention, Libya is a potent rival to Algeria, although its resources and military power and potential are probably not up to the task over the longer term. Perhaps for this reason, Libya has been at the forefront in pursuit of nuclear, chemical, biological, and ballistic missile systems, as well as longer-range aircraft. Libya's rationale for proliferation is also more closely tied to confrontation with the West than with regional competition. In fact, the Lampedusa incident of 1986 is the only instance to date of an air attack of any sort by a North African state on European territory.[8] Nonetheless, Libya's WMD assets would be relevant in conflicts with Egypt or Tunisia.[9]

A peculiarity of security perceptions in the Maghreb is that even given the very considerable distance from the cockpit of the Arab-Israeli conflict, strategic perceptions and proliferation dynamics are driven to a great extent by Israeli capabilities. Active proliferators such as Algeria and Syria refer to the Israeli threat in justifying their programs. Even Tunisia, vulnerable to systems deployed in Libya and Algeria, has been reluctant to criticize proliferation trends in the region. Tunisians recall the Israeli air attack on the PLO headquarters at Hamman-Lif outside Tunis in 1985 in which at least 20 Tunisians died. Privately, Tunisian officials may be more concerned about

---

[8]Following the U.S. air attack on Libya of April 15, 1986, Libya launched an unsuccessful Scud missile attack against the Coast Guard–operated long-range navigation (LORAN) station on the Italian island of Lampedusa.

[9]Libya has threatened Tunisian interests and territory in the past, most notably in the Gafsa incident of 1980.

Libya's military capabilities and intentions. Publicly, in such forums as the ACRS negotiations, it is the Israeli arsenal that has shaped perceptions of WMD risks (i.e., the "right of Arab states to self-defense," the problem of "double standards," and the importance of Arab and Muslim solidarity). With the waning of the Arab-Israeli conflict, Tunisia could be at the forefront in drawing attention to the regional risks flowing from the proliferation of WMD. These risks are especially pronounced in the Tunisian case: Tunis would look to Western intervention in the event of a Libyan attack, and Libyan WMD capabilities complicate this picture; Tunisia's population, concentrated in highly urbanized Tunis and a handful of other cities, is highly exposed to WMD attack; and Tunisia's geography makes its territory attractive to a Libyan regime bent on posing a serious ballistic missile threat to Europe in a crisis.

Competition in the Eastern Mediterranean and the Gulf

Far more clearly than Algeria, Egypt has a longstanding claim to leadership in the Arab and Muslim worlds, including military power and potential. Cairo has been active in pursuing certain WMD programs, most notably the development of longer-range ballistic missiles, and has a relatively well-developed indigenous capacity for WMD manufacture and export. Egypt's WMD ambitions are closely linked to its preeminent regional role and its security concerns. The latter include the military balance with Israel, despite the Camp David agreement, and the potential for conflict with Libya, whose WMD capabilities Cairo will obviously wish to deter.[10] With the increasing range of missile systems deployed in the Gulf region, Egypt as a leading "Western-oriented" Arab state will also find itself exposed to the retaliatory consequences of support for Western actions on the pattern of the Gulf War. The importance of the Suez Canal to Western power projection in the Gulf places Egypt in a particularly difficult position—one likely to become more difficult still with the growth of the Islamist movement in the country. Indeed, the prospect of an Islamic regime in Cairo, while not as clear a possibility

---

[10]Egypt has led the charge against Israel's failure to adhere to the NPT. Indeed, the NPT issue has become something of an obsession with Egyptian diplomats and military officials. Israel, for its part, has been critical of Cairo's chemical-weapons program.

as in the Algerian case, cannot be ruled out over the next decade, with serious implications for the future pace and orientation of Egypt's WMD programs.

Beyond the continuing strategic confrontation with Israel, Syria's broad involvement in Middle Eastern politics, including support for insurgents and terrorist groups operating throughout the region and elsewhere, gives Damascus a strong interest in WMD capabilities. In particular, Syrian involvement in Lebanon and its effect on Israeli security, and support for the PKK (Kurdish Workers Party) in Turkey, open the possibility of retaliatory action from Jerusalem and Ankara. WMD capabilities, especially ballistic missiles capable of reaching either country, presumably serve as a deterrent to strikes aimed at Syria proper. These are examples of a more general thrust in Syria's foreign and security policy: A high-risk game of leverage and competition with powerful neighbors puts a premium on regional deterrence. The fact that Syrian Scud-Cs—not to mention more capable systems being explored with East Asian suppliers—could reach central Anatolia is becoming a tangible factor in Turkish calculations.[11]

Iraqi WMD capabilities were similarly tied to regional ambitions and, in the first instance, strategy toward Iran. The "War of the Cities" during the Iran-Iraq War, in which both sides sought to terrorize civilian populations through indiscriminate Scud attacks, can be seen as a precursor to Saddam Hussein's Scud campaign during the Gulf conflict.[12] In both instances, the ability to demonstrate to one's own population, as well as to other countries, the vulnerability of the opponent's territory was at least as important as any specific effect on the outcome of the conflict. Baghdad's use of chemical weapons in the war against Iran can be understood more simply as a tactical gambit aimed at breaking a bloody deadlock on the ground. But taken together with the apparent use of chemicals against the Kurds

---

[11]Turkey's prime minister, Tansu Ciller, has referred to proliferation as one of NATO's "most serious problems." See Tansu Ciller, "Turkey and NATO," *NATO Review*, April 1994, p. 3. A thorough survey of Turkish thinking on nuclear proliferation in relation to regional security may be found in Doygu Sezer, *Turkey's New Security Environment, Nuclear Weapons and Proliferation,* Los Alamos: Center for National Security Studies, 1994.

[12]On the Scud attacks in the Iran-Iraq War, see Anthony H. Cordesman, *Weapons of Mass Destruction in the Middle East,* London: Brassey's, 1991, pp. 40–42.

in northern Iraq, it demonstrates an acceptance of WMD use as a "normal" aspect of warfare, quite removed from the West's view of chemical weapons as taboo. Iraq's extensive WMD ambitions have been frozen as a result of its Gulf defeat. Over the longer term, and in the absence of international sanctions on Iraq, Baghdad would almost certainly seek to rebuild its WMD capacity, not least as a response to programs in Iran and, reportedly, in Saudi Arabia.

Iran has very powerful motives for acquiring WMD and the means for their delivery at longer range. At the broadest level, the regime is interested in the ability of high-technology programs to bolster its international standing and support its role as the leading exponent of Islamist revolution. As with other leading proliferators, the ability of the Iranian military to integrate and maintain sophisticated weapon systems is doubtful. But in the case of WMD capabilities, both actual and "virtual," this consideration is largely irrelevant. It is the mere potential for havoc implied by Iran's acquisition of ex-Soviet submarines or Backfire bombers that is meaningful for international security, even if these assets prove difficult or impossible to employ with concerted effect. These systems and, in a much more dramatic way, nuclear and ballistic missile programs give Tehran considerable geostrategic weight in its regional relations as well as its dealings with powers as distant as the United States and Russia. For a state with pretensions to becoming a regional great power, the ability to threaten (in theory) population centers as distant as Paris or Moscow is a considerable asset. Similarly, Iran's ability to continue in its role as the leading rejectionist state in the conflict with Israel is reinforced by its capacity to threaten Israeli territory directly.

In the new geopolitics of the Middle East, the spread of longer-range weapons will enable states at some remove from centers of conflict to play a role in events far from their own borders, and not just in relation to the waning Arab-Israeli dispute. In short, with WMD it is no longer necessary to be a "front-line state" to make one's weight felt. In future crises, Iran and Iraq will be able to influence Cairo, Amman, and Ankara. Syria, Egypt, Libya, or Algeria might hold at risk targets in the Gulf. Similar political blackmail might be practiced against Western Europe in periods of crisis. The prospect of extending and magnifying a state's regional leverage provides a powerful incentive for the acquisition of WMD and associated delivery systems.

Finally, many of the leading proliferators have direct experience of Western intervention, in the colonial period or in recent crises. From the Suez crisis of 1956 to the renewed U.S. air strikes against Baghdad following allegations of Iraqi plans to assassinate former President Bush, regional actors on Europe's southern periphery have regularly been exposed to the retaliatory capability of the West. Western, especially American, power projection capabilities are a permanently operating factor in the strategic calculations of states as varied as Algeria, Libya, Syria, Iraq, and Iran. The possession of a deterrent capability, however weak or illusory, has considerable appeal to regimes whose external policies are strongly at variance with Western interests. As Muammar Qadhafi has stated, "If at the time of the 1986 U.S. raid on Tripoli we had possessed a deterrent missile that could reach New York, we could have hit it at the same moment."[13] Given Qadhafi's actual missile attack on Lampedusa in retaliation for this raid, neither his comment nor his presumed willingness to attack European targets closer at hand can be dismissed out of hand. Moreover, arguments about American and European sensitivity to casualties and the consequent reluctance to intervene are taken seriously—perhaps even more seriously—in North Africa and the Middle East. In this context, the possession of WMD capable of inflicting casualties in rear areas, even in the West itself, cannot fail to be attractive. The experience of the Gulf War has probably reinforced awareness of the utility of WMD, along the lines reportedly suggested by a senior Indian military official: "Don't fight the United States unless you have nuclear weapons."[14]

STRUCTURAL MOTIVES: BUREAUCRATIC AND CIVIL-MILITARY POLITICS

The internal environment in key countries of North Africa and the Levant also contributes to proliferation dynamics. The obsession with security, both internal and external, gives the military and

---

[13]As quoted in *FBIS-MEA*, April 23, 1990; also cited in Uzi Rubin, "How Much Does Missile Proliferation Matter?" *Orbis*, Winter 1991.

[14]An analysis of the perceived lessons of the Gulf War, including those drawn by Third World states, can be found in Patrick J. Garrity, *Why the Gulf War Still Matters: Foreign Perspectives on the War and the Future of International Security*, Los Alamos: Center for National Security Studies, 1993.

associated industrial establishments considerable weight. State-directed development and purchasing programs for military technology, nuclear research, and dual-use chemical facilities offer high-prestige vehicles for individual and bureaucratic activity. The international contacts, funding, and influence associated with these efforts can produce considerable momentum, giving military technology programs a life of their own. This has almost certainly been a key factor in the Algerian case, where the nuclear power program became a leading source of prestige and patronage for the military-backed FLN (National Liberation Front) bureaucracy. It would very likely serve a similar function for a successor regime in Algiers, whether Islamist or secular.[15]

One consequence of the bureaucratic momentum behind WMD programs may be resistance to unilateral or multilateral arms control. Even in cases where governments are persuaded of the need to rein in WMD programs for reasons of regional or international politics, military and industrial establishments may balk or argue for clandestine approaches. Governments, too, faced with unemployed or underemployed technicians—many trained at considerable expense abroad—may find it politically undesirable to wind down development programs.

Beyond the question of motives, potential proliferators may also see opportunities in the apparent availability of Russian and Eastern European personnel familiar with WMD technologies. This factor, as much as the potential traffic in nuclear and other materials, could stimulate interest in WMD programs where indigenous capabilities are lacking. Arguably, this potential export of material and expertise will only serve to augment resources already available on a commercial basis from China, North Korea, and, sometimes, Western Europe. When economic interests clash with security imperatives, supplier agencies tempted by the former often end up undercutting the latter. This is especially true when supplier agencies are independent of the state or when the state itself is in such economic distress (as in Russia) that near-term economic considerations tend to overwhelm longer-term security concerns. It is thus ironic that

---

[15]The evolution of military establishments and military technology in Middle Eastern states is explored in V. J. Parry and M. E. Yapp (eds.), *War, Technology and Society in the Middle East*, London: Oxford University Press, 1975.

supplier states eventually may end up being threatened by the very recipients of the current largesse—a product of either their inability or their unwillingness to control critical technology flows.

VIRTUAL VERSUS ACTUAL CAPABILITIES

If the motives for acquiring WMD capabilities are tied to the desire for systemic and regional weight, how much of this weight can be achieved short of actual possession and deployment of WMD systems? Do regimes in Algeria, Libya, or Iran, for example, actually need to build and deploy nuclear weapons, or will most of the potential gains in terms of prestige and leverage be realized through slow progress in this direction (the North Korean model)? Construction and deployment carry the risk of eliciting preemption and/or the emergence of countervailing WMD alliances, with the West or among regional competitors. Nuclear programs in particular are complex, long-term undertakings. The difficult and risky choices with regard to construction and deployment may seem remote and easily deferred at the outset. Put another way, a country such as Algeria may not be capable of producing nuclear weapons without unacceptable costs and risks. But even short of this, Algeria's fledgling nuclear program confers substantial near-term benefits in terms of prestige and political attention.

Given the importance of regional fears and ambitions in stimulating WMD programs, however, "virtual" proliferation may not be enough. As regional competitors pursue unconventional weapons and the means for their delivery, states may be pushed toward the realization of capabilities—driven along the proliferation spectrum in the face of mounting costs and risks. Libya and Algeria both house a variety of half-formed WMD efforts. Under stable conditions, many of these efforts might remain incomplete. In the face of a more serious competition for political-military position in North Africa, perhaps in the wake of a second revolution in Algiers, the perceived advantages of moving forward with difficult and expensive programs may outweigh the political and economic costs.

The search for prestige on the international and regional levels, as well as bureaucratic politics within regimes, may encourage the acquisition of weapons of mass destruction. But the emphasis on prestige rather than strategic purpose and warfighting ability may have an important influence on WMD programs. Proliferators in North Africa and the Levant are also likely to be far less interested in investing in the survivability of WMD assets, especially where hardening and mobility do not contribute to prestige and regional weight.[16]

---

[16]As noted by Scott Sagan in an informal 1993 seminar at RAND.

Chapter Three

STRATEGIC CONSEQUENCES OF WMD PROLIFERATION ON EUROPE'S SOUTHERN PERIPHERY

The spread of WMD capabilities across the Mediterranean and its hinterlands could transform the way policymakers and strategists on both sides of the Atlantic think about European and Middle Eastern security. Several issues are worth highlighting in this context: First, the question of the most likely targets for WMD use; second, the effect of WMD proliferation beyond Europe for security in Europe's regions and Allied responses; and third, the strategic and operational implications for Western freedom of action in the Middle East as a whole.

LIKELIHOOD AND VICTIMS OF WMD USE

The current "reach" of weapons of mass destruction deployed in North Africa and the Levant—for the moment, conventional or chemical, possibly biological or radiological, weapons delivered by missile, aircraft, or artillery—suggests that regional neighbors are the most likely victims of WMD use. When the overwhelming significance of regional rivalries in stimulating WMD proliferation is taken into account, the prevailing South-South character of the WMD threat is even more apparent.

Recent history points to the relatively free use of ballistic missiles in regional conflicts within the south, including Afghanistan, Iraq-Iran, the Gulf War, and most recently Yemen. The only corresponding example of an attack on Western territory is the failed Libyan attack on Lampedusa in 1986 (though one might also view the Iraqi Scud attacks on Israel and Saudi Arabia as attacks on "Western" targets). Alleged instances of chemical use have also been in a South-South context. Looking ahead, regional actors in the south are still the most likely victims of WMD use. But two qualifications are necessary here. First, the South-South character of WMD risk in the Mediterranean region may be transient. As ballistic missile systems of trans-Mediterranean range (e.g., the North Korean Nodong variants) become available, Europe will increasingly be exposed to WMD risks from the south. Indeed, many parts of southern Europe are already within range of aircraft deployed in North Africa, and Turkey is fully exposed to air and missile risks on its Middle Eastern borders. Second, political turmoil in North Africa could well result in a general deterioration of relations between Europe and its unstable periphery. Against this background, Europe's growing exposure in theory could become vulnerability in practice.

In this context, the U.S. military presence in the Mediterranean could provide both a pretext and a target for attack. It is difficult to predict with any certainty the level of U.S. military presence in central Europe over the next decade. But even if the presence shrinks to token levels or disappears entirely, it is reasonable to assume that the United States will maintain a significant naval, air, and marine presence in the Mediterranean. As ballistic and cruise missiles deployed in North Africa and the Levant acquire greater range and accuracy, these forces will be increasingly vulnerable. At a minimum, proliferators around the Mediterranean will *assume* that they are vulnerable. Moreover, the residual U.S. presence in the Mediterranean will not be aimed simply or even primarily at bolstering stability on Europe's immediate periphery. These forces will be relevant to, and very likely employed in, future contingencies in the greater Middle East. As a result, the pretext for an attack on U.S. forces in the Mediterranean will exist for regimes in North Africa and the Levant that may wish to demonstrate their solidarity with "victims" of Western aggression in the Gulf or elsewhere.

WMD AND SECURITY IN EUROPE'S REGIONS

From Portugal to Ankara, security perceptions and plans among NATO's southern allies are beginning to reflect proliferation risks emanating from the southern shores of the Mediterranean, including vulnerability to WMD. Viewed as a whole, the weight of WMD issues in security debates and policies varies considerably across the region.

In France, accustomed to WMD issues as a consequence of its own nuclear and missile capabilities, the debate and response are most advanced. Spain and Italy have devoted considerable attention to WMD trends with less attention to the problem of responses. Portugal and Greece lag behind, although concern is growing. Despite Turkey's pronounced exposure to proliferation risks, the Turkish debate has been somewhat slow in emerging but is now becoming more active.

In the western Mediterranean, European perceptions of WMD vulnerability and its meaning for regional security focus on Libya and Algeria. The former is a longstanding proliferator with a demonstrated willingness to employ weapons against European targets. The rhetoric of the Qadhafi regime with regard to the acquisition of advanced means of "self-defense" and "deterrent" capabilities has also been troubling to European officials and analysts; the regime is on record as having threatened to attack southern European territory (Spain, Italy, Greece) in the event that facilities in these countries are used to support U.S. action against Libya.[1] During the Gulf crisis, Spanish and Portuguese observers worried about reports that Iraq might have established ballistic missile test sites in Mauritania, posing a threat to Madeira and the Canaries.

The Gulf War was a watershed in terms of southern European concerns, with widespread popular support for Iraq across North Africa, as well as the experience of the Scud missile attacks on Israel and Saudi Arabia, pointing to the possibility of more proximate risks to European territory in the future. Against this background, revelations on Algeria's nuclear program and possible cooperation with Iraq, reports of Libyan interest in nuclear technology and materials from the former communist bloc, and the appearance of 1,000-km-plus missile systems on the world market have produced anxiety among strategists and policymakers. Above all, West European governments are concerned about the confluence of WMD proliferation and the possibility of a radical Islamist takeover in Algeria, with negative implications for stability from Rabat to Cairo. Even short of

---

[1]"Foreign Ministry Reacts to Al-Qadhaffi Threats," *FBIS-West Europe Report*, July 29, 1991, p. 21. See also Martin Navias, "Is There an Emerging Third World Ballistic Missile Threat to Europe?" *RUSI Journal*, Winter 1990; and "Al-Qadhaffi Loyalty Day Speech Lambasts Embargo," *FBIS-NES*, October 1, 1992, p. 9.

the advent of missile systems capable of reaching southern European cities, the possibility of conventional air attack as well as the unconventional delivery of chemical, biological, or radiological weapons by terrorists based in North Africa cannot be dismissed.[2] The security of Tunisia in the face of potential Libyan aggression is of special concern, since the deployment of mobile Libyan missiles in northern Tunisia would allow even the current Libyan systems to reach European territory.

Spain, France, and Italy have launched initiatives aimed at improving strategic and operational intelligence in the Mediterranean, notably the Helios satellite surveillance system.[3] These three countries are also actively pursuing initiatives aimed at improving air defense and, ultimately, anti-ballistic-missile capabilities. Notable developments in this area include Spanish integration into NATO and European air defense networks, and the Franco-Italian EUROSAM consortium aimed at developing a multirole European air defense system.

Traditional French and southern European opposition to the concept of strategic defenses has all but evaporated in the wake of the Gulf War. Prominent observers such as Francois Heisbourg and Henri Coze have pointed to the wisdom of French investments in ATBM capabilities in the context of southern Mediterranean risks.[4]

Given the political constraints associated with threatening the use of nuclear forces against North African targets, French planning now favors the search for conventional means of preemption and deterrence in relation to WMD risks in the south. In particular, France is seeking to strengthen its capacity for discrete targeting and precision

---

[2]See "France Studies Non-Nuclear Deterrence," *International Defense Review*, February 1993, pp. 92–93.

[3]Helios is an optical reconnaissance satellite designed to provide imagery of specific sites daily. Depending on the height of the orbit, it can provide imagery at 12- or 24-hour intervals. Subsequent satellites will be equipped with infrared as well as optical equipment. Alasdair McLean, "European Military Space Programs," *Military Technology*, May 1992, p. 17.

[4]On the French debate over southern risks, see Margaret Blunden, "France After the Cold War: Inching Closer to the Alliance," *Defence Analysis*, Vol. 9, No. 3, pp. 259–270. France and Italy are codeveloping the Syrinx SAM system for ATBM interception. See Duncan Lennox, "ATBMs and Beyond," *Jane's Defence Weekly*, May 22, 1993, p. 21.

strike of WMD-related facilities, delivery systems, and command centers.[5]

French policymakers may well see proliferation risks and the desire for coordination on air defense and ATBM systems as incentives for more active participation in NATO planning, in addition to established patterns of European and bilateral cooperation. For Portugal, Spain, and Italy, deepening concern over the vulnerability of their territory and interests in the Mediterranean region, coupled with limited resources for defense, suggests a continuing interest in cooperation to address WMD. This approach is already observable in the multilateral initiatives outlined above. It is also likely to give these southern European countries, as well as Greece and Turkey, a stake in NATO counterproliferation efforts. The Alliance "policy framework" on proliferation of weapons of mass destruction, issued by the North Atlantic Council in Istanbul, refers explicitly to the risk of "allies being threatened by an adversary that obtained WMD capabilities developed in areas beyond NATO's periphery."[6]

Instability in Algeria, and fears of its consequences across North Africa, will almost certainly place proliferation risks in the western Mediterranean in a more dangerous light. The advent of a radical Islamic regime in Algiers (this is not the only possible outcome) might affect proliferation dynamics. More significantly, it might also deepen existing conflicts over political, economic, and territorial questions (e.g., Spanish-Moroccan friction over the sovereignty of Ceuta and Melilla, and separatism in the Canary Islands).

In the eastern Mediterranean and its hinterlands, the spread of WMD and the current concern about WMD risks affect regional security perceptions in several ways. First and most dramatically, proliferation trends in the Middle East have already transformed the strategic environment on Turkey's borders. Even during the Gulf War, Ankara sought NATO reassurance against the threat of Iraqi missile attacks

---

[5]Highly accurate air-to-surface missile are the most promising weapons for this role. See "France Studies Non-Nuclear Deterrence," *International Defense Review*, February 1993, pp. 92–93.

[6]"Alliance Policy Framework on Proliferation of Weapons of Mass Destruction," issued at the Ministerial Meeting of the North Atlantic Council, Istanbul, June 9, 1994. Published in *NATO Review*, June 1994, pp. 28–29.

on population centers in southeast Turkey. Since that period, Turkish strategists have become increasingly concerned about the threat posed to Turkish territory by modified Scud and more-advanced missile systems deployed or under development by Syria and Iran. Despite the substantial qualitative and quantitative improvements in its defense capability since the Gulf War, Turkey's vulnerability to threats from these quarters has grown. Ankara continues to press for permanent deployment of Patriot air defense batteries, and the entire subject of counterproliferation policy is emerging as a special interest of Turkey within NATO. (It is appropriate and hardly coincidental that the alliance policy framework on WMD proliferation was presented in Istanbul.) Considering Ankara's active disputes with Iran, Iraq, and Syria, the proliferation problem on Turkey's Middle Eastern borders is not simply theoretical. Indeed, U.S. and Alliance policy with regard to the defense of Turkey against WMD attack may well emerge as a *sine qua non* for Turkish security cooperation in other areas.

Turkey's exposure to WMD risks on its borders may also affect military balances and strategic perceptions in the Balkans, a notable example of Middle Eastern WMD risks spilling over into adjacent European theaters. If Turkey is unable to insure itself against proliferation risks in an Alliance framework—as a result of inadequate NATO initiatives in this area or the deterioration of Turkish relations within the Alliance—it will very likely seek to acquire the means of defense or deterrence on a unilateral basis. This would almost certainly be the case in the missile arena, and ultimately it could apply to the development of nuclear weapons. This would, in turn, have a very significant effect on strategic perceptions in the Balkans, where Turkey's role is already a subject of some sensitivity. Indeed, Greek strategists speculate on the dire consequence that a nuclear Iran might well cause Turkey to explore the nuclear option. More farfetched, but hardly inconceivable, would be the ability of a WMD-armed Iran (or even an Iran capable of reaching central Europe with conventionally armed ballistic missiles) to *threaten* attacks on behalf of Muslim interests in the Balkans.

Counterproliferation policy is clearly set to emerge as an area of keen interest for NATO, as well as future cooperation among Allied states. But there will also be considerable potential for friction as NATO seeks to redefine itself after the Cold War, especially given likely variations in vulnerability to WMD attack across the Alliance. The prospect of near-term southern European vulnerability to missiles based on the European periphery, while northern and central Europe remain relatively (for the moment) out of range, could introduce serious strains in considering Alliance policies for deterrence and defense.[7] Some allies will have an incentive to spread WMD risks to the extent possible. Others, further north, will wish to minimize their exposure. This problem could be even more pronounced beyond NATO, in relation to the WEU and European defense efforts. Europeans, already wary of the security baggage that full Turkish membership in the EU or WEU might imply, will be even more wary of acquiring new defense commitments in the Middle East as a result of pressing proliferation risks on Turkey's borders.

Overall, it is a striking irony that southern Europe and the Mediterranean, the least nuclear of theaters during the Cold War, has emerged as a leading, perhaps *the* leading, center of nuclear and other WMD risks in the new strategic environment.

IMPLICATIONS FOR U.S. AND WESTERN FREEDOM OF ACTION

Proliferation trends on Europe's southern periphery will exert a considerable influence on the freedom of action of the United States and its NATO allies, especially in relation to North African and Middle Eastern contingencies.[8] The implications may be traced at three levels: (1) growing interdependence of European and Middle Eastern security; (2) resulting effects on security cooperation in crises; and (3) influence on propensity and ease of Western intervention, and the emergence of new classes of contingencies and targets.

---

[7]Roger Molander, "Proliferation of Weapons of Mass Destruction and Implications for Mediterranean Regional Security," in Ian Lesser and Robert Levine (eds.), *RAND/ Istituto Affari Internazionali Conference on the New Mediterranean Security Environment: Conference Proceedings,* Santa Monica, CA: RAND, CF-110-RC, 1993.

[8]An important thrust of this analysis is that proliferators need not be able to strike at U.S. territory in order to threaten U.S. interests and affect U.S. freedom of action. For an argument minimizing the ballistic missile risk to the United States, see Lora Lumpe, Lisbeth Gronlund, and David C. Wright, "Third World Missiles Fall Short," *Bulletin of the Atomic Scientists*, March 1992.

As the foregoing analysis suggests, one consequence of the spread of WMD along the European periphery is likely to be the progressive confluence of the European and Middle Eastern security environments. Instability on Europe's southern periphery will affect the prosperity and security of European societies, and will require Western presence and involvement—political, economic, and military. With the proliferation of weapon systems of increasing range along the southern and eastern shores of the Mediterranean, European territory will be exposed, in a more or less direct manner, to the consequences of North-South frictions and Western intervention. This will represent a considerable deepening of the exposure that already exists in the form of international terrorist action on European soil. The chance that weapons of mass destruction might actually be used against European targets—or American forces in and around Europe—may remain small. But the very possibility of, for example, Libyan, Syrian, or Algerian retaliation will influence the prospects for European intervention in the Middle East. It may also influence patterns of transatlantic cooperation in Middle Eastern contingencies.

This second implication is of considerable importance in considering the freedom of action the United States is likely to enjoy in conducting military operations in North Africa and the Gulf. Contemplation of a new intervention on the pattern of the Desert Shield/Desert Storm operations, but with one or more North African states in possession of even conventionally armed ballistic missiles of trans-Mediterranean range, illustrates the sort of challenges that can be expected in the future. Some 40 percent of U.S. deployments in response to crisis since 1945 have been to or through the Mediterranean.[9] During the Gulf War, some 90 percent of the forces and materiel sent to the Gulf passed through the Mediterranean region, by air or sea.[10] Access to southern European bases and airspace played an important role in coalition force projection. Facilities in Spain and Turkey, among others, contributed to the conduct of the air war against Iraq. Southern European states, as well as France,

---

[9]Comment by General John Galvin, quoted in Ian Kemp, "USAF Quits Spain: New Base in Doubt," *Jane's Defence Weekly*, August 3, 1991, p. 177.

[10]AFSOUTH estimate, cited in "Draft Interim Report of the Sub-Committee on the Southern Region," North Atlantic Assembly, 1991, p. 10. See also Admiral Jonathan T. Howe, "NATO and the Gulf Crisis," *Survival*, May/June 1991, p. 247.

contributed forces to the ground, sea, and air operations in the Gulf. Turkey, on the front line against Iraq, supported coalition operations in various ways, any of which might have elicited an Iraqi response. The prospect of Iraqi retaliation against coalition population centers would almost certainly have produced a very different calculus of cooperation in Europe. Again, looking ahead, if one posits more radical North African states armed with 1,000-km ballistic missiles, the incentives for caution on the part of European states will increase even further (Libya's WMD ambitions and rhetoric, and the possibility of an Islamic regime in Algiers, suggest that this scenario is far from unlikely). European allies, including states such as Portugal, Spain, Italy, and Greece, which lack well-developed national means of deterring WMD attacks, might still offer access to bases and airspace, or contribute forces based on strong collective interest. But dialogue with the United States on these matters will be very different if Madrid, Nice, or Naples are clearly at risk.

At a minimum, the United States and NATO will pay a political and operational price for securing European, especially southern European and Turkish, cooperation under conditions of WMD threat. In some cases, allied support may have to be hidden, a requirement that would run counter to prevailing ideas about consensus building and multilateralism. In near-term crises, southern European countries will almost certainly require deployment of ATBM and air defense assets on or around their territory (regardless of effectiveness) in order to reassure parliaments and publics. Over the longer term, development and deployment of truly effective ATBM defenses—perhaps sea based and capable of deployment around the Mediterranean—may be a prerequisite for NATO engagement outside Europe. Similarly, there may be demands for a new U.S. doctrine of extended deterrence in the context of WMD risks emanating from outside Europe. To the extent that resources for the conduct of mid-scale regional contingencies decline, the need for substantial European involvement in the defense of Western interests in the Gulf and elsewhere is likely to grow, making these issues of deterrence and reassurance even more critical for U.S. policymakers and planners.

In operational terms, the growth of WMD capabilities in countries against which the West may find itself in open conflict, as well as in "rear" areas such as North Africa, will influence the propensity for and the timing, character, and duration of intervention. The *poten-*

tial for retaliation on NATO territory, possibly from unexpected quarters, will influence the basic, initial calculations on the wisdom of intervention, especially in marginal cases. Once the decision to act is taken, WMD risks may influence the choice of instruments. This is likely to be a complex equation: the risk of chemical, biological, or nuclear attack might argue for the use of air power wherever possible, to minimize the vulnerability of ground forces. On the other hand, the air attack of strategic targets might only serve to provoke retaliatory attacks on allied population centers within the range of enemy air and missile forces. Under these conditions, serious disagreements among allies may emerge about the choice of instruments and targets, based on varying exposure to WMD attack.[11]

A full discussion of the effects of WMD on the operational environment, not to mention the implications for training, equipment, and doctrine, is clearly beyond the scope of this report. But critical issues in this context will certainly include the following: The proportion of air and ballistic missile defense assets attached to intervention forces, and their location; the potential inability or unwillingness of some coalition partners to deploy forces in theaters where WMD are present and likely to be used; the undesirability of concentrating forces in rear areas, including ports and airfields; approaches aimed at minimizing or concealing the exposure of forces over time; and finally, the increased importance of disengagement strategies.

In the Mediterranean context, three issues will be of special significance for U.S. strategy and operations. First is the question of the exposure of U.S. forces in the Mediterranean or based at facilities in southern Europe and Turkey. The growing prominence of security risks along Europe's southern periphery, as well as the utility of U.S. forces in the region for power projection beyond the Mediterranean basin, suggest that the United States will wish to retain a significant forward presence to Europe's south. And for the moment, the relatively inaccurate missile systems deployed by or available to Mediterranean states are of limited utility in striking military targets. But U.S. forces based in the Mediterranean may already be vulnerable to unconventional delivery systems, and over time the accuracy of

---

[11]One can well imagine, for example, the disputes that might emerge among French, British, Italian, and U.S. officials on the subjects of deterrence, preemption, nuclear versus conventional responses, etc.

missile systems available to Third World states will undoubtedly improve. It is therefore possible that a combination of growing exposure and growing host-country concern about becoming WMD targets as a result of the U.S. presence will work to encourage further reductions in the level of permanent U.S. presence at facilities around the Mediterranean (e.g., in Spain, Italy, and Turkey, and on Crete). These pressures should, however, be offset by the requirements for deterrence and defense in the south; requirements that may not be met as effectively without a substantial permanent presence.

A second key issue concerns the size and composition of forces that may need to be kept in the Mediterranean—or deployed in Turkey—for purposes of reassurance and deterrence during potential operations in the Gulf. The Gulf War saw considerable air and naval forces deployed in the Mediterranean, partly to insure against risks emanating from Libya or threats to Suez, partly for reasons of Alliance politics.[12] With the spread of WMD capabilities, the problem of deterring and defending against "extended" retaliation by anti-Western regimes closer to Europe will become more acute. In an era of shrinking forces, this could prove a costly distraction. It may also be a promising area for improvement of European capabilities, on the pattern of national and multinational initiatives already under way, and as a contribution to burden sharing in defense of Western interests in the Gulf.

The prospect of continuing WMD proliferation around the Mediterranean suggests a new class of contingencies, in which force may be threatened or employed for purposes of dissuasion, preemption, or retaliation in relation to WMD. These missions will undoubtedly pose daunting challenges for strategic and tactical intelligence and precision strike of mobile or hardened targets. In the case of unconventional delivery systems, perhaps under the control of substate actors, additional challenges would arise. Moreover, all of these factors will come into play in a multilateral context, raising complex issues of political consensus, intelligence sharing, command and control, and so forth. More positively, it should be noted that the Mediter-

---

[12]For example, a large proportion of the German surface fleet was deployed to the Mediterranean during the Gulf crisis. Deployment to the Gulf would have raised more complex political issues both inside and outside Germany.

ranean continues to be an area of extensive and regular military co-operation among the NATO allies, including those members outside the Alliance's integrated command structure (France and Spain). Much useful infrastructure as well as a habit of cooperation already exist in the region. Given a basic consensus on WMD risks and responses, there is a strong basis for bilateral and multilateral cooperation on the military aspects of counterproliferation.

Finally, it should be remembered that nonmilitary policies are likely to play the leading role in containing proliferation pressures around the Mediterranean. As this analysis suggests, the motives for proliferation in the region are closely bound up with perceptions of insecurity among states in the south, and the continuing search for prestige and geopolitical weight. In a deeper sense, it is the pressure for internal political and economic change across North Africa and the Middle East that threatens the stability of regimes and encourages aggressive external behavior. Global efforts to restrict the spread of WMD, in the form of nonproliferation and supplier agreements as well as pressure on Western and non-Western sources of weapons and technology, will be highly relevant to the Mediterranean. Equally important, however, will be the range of European and U.S. policies aimed at promoting peaceful change within societies on Europe's southern periphery, as well as North-South security dialogue.[13] Countries insecure and adrift are far more likely to find a strategic rationale for acquiring weapons capable of influencing their relationship with neighbors on both sides of the Mediterranean.

----

[13]Prominent examples include the Euro-Mediterranean Initiative, embracing economic, cultural and political-security issues, and NATO's emerging Mediterranean initiative, aimed at fostering security dialogue between the Alliance and six nonmember Mediterranean states (Mauritania, Morocco, Tunisia, Egypt, Israel, and Jordan). Unfortunately, the leading proliferators (Libya and Iran) are, almost by definition, unacceptable partners for dialogue.

Chapter Four

CONCLUSIONS

The analysis of proliferation trends and regional security consequences suggests the following conclusions and implications for U.S. policy and strategy.

STATUS AND TRENDS

Many of the world's leading WMD proliferators are arrayed along Europe's southern periphery, and WMD risks are transforming the security environment in the Mediterranean as well as in Europe's regions. Key states south and east of the Mediterranean either possess or are in the process of acquiring WMDs, along with the means for delivering them across the Mediterranean. Iran already has a substantial chemical-weapons capability and is pursuing nuclear and biological capabilities. It has an active long-range ballistic missile development program and has moved toward acquiring significant numbers of deep-strike aircraft (a WMD delivery system that is often overlooked). Iraq's weapon programs are on hold while UN sanctions prevail, but Baghdad is in a position to develop chemical and biological weapons quickly once those sanctions are lifted. Egypt also has active chemical-weapons and long-range missile development programs.

Both Libya and Syria have chemical weapons (Libya also has a biological capability), and Algeria has been pushing ahead with development of a nuclear infrastructure. Like Iran, Iraq, and Egypt, all three countries have received help in developing or acquiring both WMDs and delivery systems from external sources such as China and North Korea. Unlike Iran, Iraq, and Egypt, the countries farther to the west do not yet have the indigenous industrial base needed to pursue such weapon systems on their own. They are thus more dependent on their supplier network, but the risks posed by Libya and Syria (and potentially Algeria) are nonetheless real for at least as long as that network lasts.

Within ten years, it is possible that every southern European capital will be within range of ballistic missiles based in North Africa or the Levant. Turkish population centers are already exposed to missiles based in Syria and Iran (and Iraq). Southern European, French, and Turkish security debates and policies are being influenced to a considerable degree by the perception of risks emanating from the south (in the Turkish case, from the Middle East), above all proliferation risks. In some instances, perceptions have outstripped the reality of system ranges and capabilities. But proliferation trends suggest that European concerns may soon be justified.

Political turmoil in North Africa and the greater Middle East reinforces proliferation risks in the Mediterranean. The potential advent of a radical Islamic regime in Algeria, with its nuclear ambitions and missile interests, could accelerate proliferation trends across North Africa and worsen the outlook for WMD threats in times of crisis. Violent political change in North Africa could encourage broader WMD-based alliances in the Middle East (Algeria-Syria-Iran, for instance), compounding the proliferation challenge.

WMD proliferation in North Africa and the Levant will continue to be fueled by systemic, regional, and internal motives. Key regional actors, including Algeria, Libya, Egypt, Syria, and Iran, are engaged in an active search for geopolitical "weight" and national prestige in the post–Cold War world. Even modest WMD capabilities or the mere pursuit of such capabilities are seen as contributing to these states' ability to be taken seriously in Muslim, Arab, and "Southern" circles, and on the international scene as a whole. At the same time, regional frictions and multiple internal and external challenges provide motives for proliferation.

The spread of WMD and longer-range delivery systems suggests that traditional distinctions between European and Middle Eastern security are eroding. Europe is increasingly exposed to the retaliatory consequences of Western—especially U.S.—action beyond Europe.

Hints of this development could be seen in the Persian Gulf experience, when the popular reaction in North Africa and the potential for terrorist attacks on European soil were matters of concern, especially to southern Europeans. In future crises of this nature, the proliferation of WMD and longer-range delivery systems will create the potential for brinkmanship, either by affected states in the Middle East or their allies in North Africa. In effect, the spread of long-range weapons enables possessor states at some remove from centers of conflict to play a role in events far from their own borders.

For the moment, however, the most pressing WMD risks are South-South, and the neighbors of proliferators in North Africa and the Levant are the most likely first victims of WMD use. The North-South dimensions of WMD proliferation could become more prominent with the spread of longer-range delivery systems and, as important, to the extent that political-military relations across the Mediterranean worsen.

IMPLICATIONS FOR POLICY AND STRATEGY

The presence of WMD will substantially complicate decisions regarding intervention beyond Europe, along with choices relating to the equipment, training, doctrine, and objectives of intervention forces. The preference for multinational operations in areas such as the Gulf and North Africa will add to this complexity, with potentially competing stakes, levels of WMD vulnerability, and capacity and tolerance for operations in a WMD environment.

Above all, the growing perception and reality of European exposure to WMD risks will affect the climate for cooperation in extra-European contingencies. The vulnerability of European population centers, especially in the context of ballistic missile threats, is likely to change the calculus of cooperation in ways that will directly affect U.S. freedom of action and the capacity for power projection. Access to bases and air space along the logistically vital Mediterranean–Indian Ocean axis will be far less predictable under these conditions. Vulnerable allies may be reluctant to commit forces or even to support U.S. action under some conditions. At a minimum, European cooperation—especially southern European and Turkish cooperation—will come at a higher political and operational price.

Specifically, countries exposed to WMD will demand greater reassurance and deterrence against these risks. This will take the form of requests for development and deployment of more capable antimissile defenses, including the preemptive deployment of Patriot-like systems in times of crisis. More active treatment of WMD issues and counterproliferation policy within NATO will almost certainly emerge as a *sine qua non* for greater Alliance out-of-area involvement. In the absence of new antimissile and counterproliferation initiatives, the prospects for unfettered access and cooperation in future Gulf-like contingencies may well decline.

Consideration should be given to specific technical and political-strategic initiatives aimed at bolstering the security of Europe (and U.S. forces operating around the Mediterranean) in the face of WMD risks. On the technical side, alternatives for mobile, rapidly deployable antimissile defenses in the Mediterranean deserve active exploration. To influence the calculus of cooperation in crises, such systems should be able to go beyond merely symbolic defense of population centers. The United States, in cooperation with key allies—not least France—should lead a reappraisal of Alliance strategy regarding WMD threats from the Middle East. Responsiveness on this issue may be just as vital to European security and the future of NATO as the successful management of more familiar challenges in the East.

The prospect of continuing WMD proliferation around the Mediterranean suggests a new class of contingencies, in which force may be required for purposes of dissuasion, preemption, or retaliation in relation to WMD. These missions will undoubtedly pose daunting challenges for strategic and tactical intelligence and precision strike of mobile or hardened targets. In the case of unconventional delivery systems, perhaps under the control of substate actors, additional challenges would arise. Moreover, all of these factors will come into play in a multilateral context, with complex issues of political consensus, intelligence sharing, command and control, etc. More positively, it should be noted that the Mediterranean continues to be an area of extensive and regular military cooperation among the NATO allies, including those members outside the Alliance's integrated command structure (France and Spain), and that much useful infrastructure as well as a habit of cooperation already exist in the region.

MASS DESTRUCTION CAPABILITIES AND DELIVERY SYSTEMS IN NORTH AFRICA AND THE LEVANT

The information catalogued in this appendix suggests that North Africa and the Levant are currently undergoing a strategic transformation as states seek to acquire various weapons of mass destruction and the long-range delivery systems required to carry them. This transformation has increased in pace in the last several years: the collapse of the bipolar order has removed the structural restraints that inhibited the transfer of highly sophisticated weapons, and the rise of Russian, Chinese, and North Korean arms-for-cash sales has ensured that technologies previously unavailable can now be purchased on the open market in exchange for hard currency. The sale of sophisticated weapon systems like the SU-24 Fencer and the MiG-29 Fulcrum to Iran is a case in point. Given the spread of conventional and nonconventional capabilities in North Africa and the Levant, it is not surprising to find analysts already inquiring as to whether we are witnessing "an emerging Third World threat to Europe."[1] The information detailed in this appendix clearly suggests that while northern and central Europe are still substantially immune to any threats emerging from North Africa and the Levant, the southern region of the continent does not enjoy similar immunity. The problems resulting from this loss of immunity will only deepen as the proliferating states increase the types and numbers of threatening weapon systems and develop the operating and logistical skills required to wield them efficiently. Against this must be weighed the

---

[1]See, by way of example, Martin Navias, "Is There an Emerging Third World Ballistic Missile Threat to Europe?" *RUSI Journal*, Winter 1990, pp. 12–16.

reality that North African and Levantic states remain the most likely first targets of WMD use.

The coercive capabilities of states in North Africa and the Levant can be divided, in general, into three separate categories.

The first category consists of states that do not possess either weapons of mass destruction or sophisticated delivery systems and show no inclination to acquire them. Unfortunately, only one state currently falls into this category: Morocco. It has no nuclear, biological, and chemical weapons (NBC) programs worth mentioning and has shown little interest in acquiring such capabilities. Moroccan delivery systems are for the most part short-legged systems, in all probability intended for use only in and around the Maghreb.

The second category consists of states that possess or seek to acquire some or all kinds of weapons of mass destruction, together with their associated delivery systems, but do not possess the requisite domestic industrial base to undertake such efforts with a high degree of autonomy. This category comprises states with essentially brittle capabilities: they seek to deploy weapons of mass destruction and operate sophisticated delivery systems but are unable to design, produce, or modify these capabilities indigenously. As a result, they rely on external assistance to a high degree and so are more vulnerable to disruptions in the supplier network. Of those examined here, the three states that best fit this category are Algeria, Libya, and Syria.

Algeria is a state whose nuclear capabilities and whose participation in the underground nuclear trade deserve continued attention well into the future. Besides Iran and Iraq, Algeria is one of the few states that has placed priority on acquiring a nuclear infrastructure. Algeria completely relies on external suppliers for its nuclear program: in the initial stages, Argentina was a participant, but the desire to avoid safeguarded nuclear arrangements may have pushed Algeria in the direction of collaboration with China. Algeria has also acquired a small number of long-range strike aircraft, though its ability to use these systems effectively is still an open question. Should Algeria expand these capabilities further, or should the state be taken over by a radical regime hostile to the West, these programs and capabilities would become a source of greater concern.

Libya represents a perennial threat largely because of its overtly hostile intentions. Libya's nuclear capabilities are minimal, but its nuclear ambitions remain undimmed despite the complete lack of achievement over the last couple of decades. Libya's chemical-biological capabilities and potential, however, are significant. The sophistication of these programs is not a consequence of indigenous skills, but rather Libya's ability to systematically evade the relevant nonproliferation regimes and recruit the assistance of European firms in developing its chemical-biological weapons complex. These programs and networks represent a serious long-term source of threat, particularly because of Libya's demonstrated willingness to use and support terror as an instrument of state policy. Moreover, Libya has both operational ballistic missiles and a long-range ballistic missile development effort, the latter heavily dependent on external assistance. Libya also has a small contingent of highly capable, deep-penetration strike aircraft and larger numbers of shorter-range dedicated ground-attack aircraft. Because Libyan proficiency in using these systems is suspect, unconventional means of WMD delivery may be the principal options in the policy-relevant future.

Syria represents the last example of a state that has or seeks to acquire weapons of mass destruction and their associated delivery systems but lacks the indigenous skills to give these capabilities any depth. Syria possesses a substantial repository of chemical capabilities in large part because manufacturing chemical weapons (or, at least, some types of them) is an easy by-product of a petrochemical infrastructure. Syria has actively sought long-range ballistic missiles, in large part because the Syrian air force has been so ineffective in penetrating its traditional adversary, Israel. The Syrian air force has a small number of deep-penetration strike aircraft, but if past history is any guide, its operational effectiveness is highly uncertain. Moreover, both aircraft and missile forces depend heavily on external assistance for their viability. The demise of the Soviet Union has forced Syria to develop a variety of relationships with North Korea, Iran, and China, relationships that could prove troublesome over the long run.

The third category consists of states that have or acquire some or all kinds of weapons of mass destruction, together with their associated delivery systems, and also have a domestic industrial base of some breadth. The presence of such a domestic base allows these states to undertake indigenous research, development, system modification, and reverse-engineering efforts. Consequently, these states acquire some degree of autonomy, a freedom of maneuver that is enhanced by their pursuit of new supplier relationships. In sum, this category identifies states with more flexible indigenous capabilities.

Egypt, the most capable state in North Africa, represents the best example of this category. Although its nuclear programs are minimal though ongoing, its chemical-weapons effort is a cause for concern. Egypt's capabilities, however, are best manifested in its long-range ballistic missile development program; after the collapse of the Argentinean Condor program, Egypt has begun collaboration with China and North Korea to produce a variety of extended-range ballistic missile programs. Egypt's indigenous programs have already resulted in the manufacture of a whole class of fairly long-range unguided battlefield rockets, and Egypt maintains a variety of highly capable combat aircraft in significant numbers. While the present Egyptian regime is allied with the United States, a future hostile regime would inherit Egypt's current R&D programs and theoretically could use them to threaten vital U.S. interests in southern Europe and Turkey.

Iraq presents a serious and long-term concern in the areas of weapons of mass destruction and long-range delivery systems. While such Iraqi capabilities are scheduled to be destroyed under the terms of the UN cease-fire resolutions, it is an open question whether the UN will actually succeed in identifying, locating, and destroying all these systems. At any rate, it is sobering to learn that according to CIA estimates, if sanctions are lifted, Iraq could produce nuclear weapons in five to seven years, restore chemical-weapons production in less than a year, and produce militarily significant quantities of biological weapons in a matter of weeks.[2] This estimate points to the real problem: Iraqi capabilities are fairly well "domesticated." The weapon systems may be destroyed in the short run, but the resource base, the pool of trained personnel, and the institutional memory cannot be erased entirely. As a result, even alternative political regimes could, if they chose to, resurrect Iraqi WMD programs at any time in the future.

---

[2]"Iraq: Defense Organization/Strength," Periscope database, July 15, 1993.

Iran, more than any other third-category state, poses the most serious potential WMD risk. Being a large country, strategically located and with significant oil resources, Iran has both the material and technical wherewithal to become a important "regional influential" worthy of notice. Iran already has a substantial chemical-weapons capability and is, increasingly, pursuing full-fledged nuclear and biological capabilities, including—as has been claimed—the outright purchase of nuclear weapons from former Soviet republics. In recent years, Iran has also moved toward acquiring significant numbers of deep strike aircraft, even while it works toward refurbishing those earlier-generation U.S. aircraft that were grounded after the revolution. The breakup of the Soviet Union and the economic distress in the various successor republics have given Iran an excellent opportunity to augment its weapons inventories with large numbers of modern delivery systems. Iran has an active long-range ballistic missile development program and is pursuing a variety of relationships with China and North Korea designed to produce both cruise and ballistic missile delivery systems. Iran will remain an important actor, among other things, because of its increasing military capabilities and because its evolving relationships with the Central Asian republics affects both Gulf and Mediterranean security.

Below we examine in detail the WMD potential of Morocco, Algeria, Libya, Egypt, Syria, Iraq, and Iran. Each country section adheres to the following organizational scheme:

- WMD potential or capabilities
    - Nuclear facilities
    - Biological facilities
    - Chemical facilities
    - Foreign collaboration and presence
- Delivery systems
    - Ballistic missiles
    - Cruise missiles
    - Aircraft
    - Artillery and battlefield rocket systems

The cutoff date for all the information that follows is January 1995.

MOROCCO

WMD Potential or Capabilities

Nuclear facilities. Morocco has a single research reactor, MA-R1, under construction. It is a Triga Mk. I–type reactor capable of producing 100,000 kW of steady power. It is operated by the CNESTN and was due to go critical sometime in 1992.

Morocco is not known to have any nuclear fuel cycle facilities.

Biological facilities. No known biological-weapons production facilities and no indications of any organized research activity.

Chemical facilities. No known chemical-weapons production facilities and no indications of any organized research activity.

Foreign collaboration and presence. The most significant foreign presence in Morocco consists of U.S., French, and Egyptian advisers. The exact numbers are unknown.

Delivery Systems[3]

Ballistic missiles. No known ballistic missiles in service or in R&D.

Cruise missiles. The Moroccan navy deploys two classes of short-range surface-to-surface cruise missiles aboard its corvettes and patrol craft. The single Spanish *Descubierta*-class frigate is fitted for, but seldom carries, four French MM-38 Exocet SSMs. The two *Assad*-class corvettes are each equipped with 3 × 2 Italian Otomat Mk. 2

---

[3]The types and numbers of all the delivery systems listed in the following pages have been derived principally from *The Military Balance, 1994–1995*. If we needed further identification of a system, we obtained it by cross-examining *The Middle East Military Balance* (various years) and the Periscope database maintained by the U.S. Naval Institute. Information about the performance of various ballistic and sea-based cruise missiles was obtained from *Jane's Strategic Weapons Systems* and *Jane's Fighting Ships* respectively.

Information about the performance of various air-launched cruise missiles was obtained from *Jane's Air-launched Weapons*. Information about the performance of aircraft was obtained from various editions of *Jane's All the World's Aircraft*. Finally, information about the performance of artillery and battlefield multiple-launch rocket systems was obtained from *Brassey's Artillery of the World* and various editions of *Jane's Armor and Artillery*.

SSMs, while the four Spanish Lazaga missile craft are each equipped with four MM-38 Exocet SSMs.

Table 1 indicates that the cruise missiles in the Moroccan inventory are essentially short-range tactical weapons designed primarily for antisurface warfare (ASUW). With the exception of the *Descubierta*-class frigate, all other launch platforms are essentially brown-water patrol craft of neither great endurance nor range. Morocco is apparently planing the acquisition of two additional *Descubierta*-class frigates as well as two more *Assad*-class corvettes, if funds permit; such an acquisition would increase Morocco's ASUW assets considerably. Both the Exocet and the Otomat missiles could theoretically be modified for a land-attack role, carrying some sort of unconventional warhead; such modifications, however, would require extensive changes to both the guidance systems and the warhead. Morocco, thus far, has not demonstrated any ability to undertake such modifications, and the lack of a nuclear, biological, and chemical research and development program in the country suggests that the prospect of such modifications would not be a concern in the foreseeable future.

Aircraft. All aircraft capable of strike and ground-attack missions are deployed with the Moroccan air force. These aircraft vary in capability from light interceptors with minimal ground-attack capability,

Table 1

Moroccan Cruise Missiles

Missile	Type	Launch Platform	Number of Platforms	Missile Range (km)	Guidance and Missile Accuracy	Type of Warhead (weight in kg)
MM-38 Exocet	SSM	Ship	5	42	Inertial with active radar	HE fragmentation (165)
Otomat Mk. 2	SSM	Ship	2	180	Inertial with command update and active radar	HE semi-armor piercing (210)

Table 2

Moroccan Combat Aircraft

Aircraft	Primary Mission	Approximate Combat Radius	Approximate Maximum Payload	Types of Weapons Carried	Number
F-5E	Fighter–ground attack	120–570 nm[a]	3,175 kg	General-purpose bombs, rockets, AAMs; ASM: AGM-65B Maverick	16
F-5F	Trainer	Same as above	Same as above	Fire-control system retained enabling weapons carriage	4
F-1E	Multirole fighter with specialized GA capability	230–750 nm	6,300 kg	AAMs: R-550 Magic, R-530; assorted general-purpose bombs and rockets	14
F-1C	Interceptor with visual GA capability	Same as above	Same as above	Same as above	15
Alpha Jet	Light attack/COIN aircraft	340–580 nm	2,500 kg	Mixed fuel, bomb and rocket loads; under-fuselage podded cannon	23
CM-170 Magister	Light attack/COIN aircraft			Rockets, AS.11 ASM	23
OV-10	Light attack/COIN aircraft	198–265 nm	1,633 kg	General-purpose bombs, rockets, AAMs	4

[a]The approximate combat radius depends, inter alia, on the type and weight of ordnance carried, the cruising profile, and the kind and number of external fuel tanks. The 120-nm combat radius presumes full ordnance load, two Sidewinder missiles, maximum internal fuel, 5 minutes of combat, and a low-low-low profile usually associated with covert ground-attack missions. The 570-nm figure, in contrast, presumes a fighter intercept mission with the aircraft carrying maximum internal fuel, two Sidewinder missiles, reserves for 20 minutes, and 5 minutes of combat with maximum engine power.

like the Northrop F-5 E/F and the French-German Alpha Jet, to the more-capable, multipurpose aircraft like the French Mirage F-1.

The most capable strike aircraft in the Moroccan air force are the 14 French Mirage F-1Es, which have an effective combat radius in the 400-nm class. Capable of carrying up to 6,300 kg of munitions, these aircraft can readily deliver payloads well beyond Madrid if based at the airfields at Tangier and Tetuan. The 15 Mirage F-1Cs have similar range and payload capacity, but they are primarily interceptors with only a visual ground-attack capability. The Alpha Jet ranks next in operational reach, with a combat radius in the 300-nm class. This aircraft, however, carries a relatively light payload and, if fully loaded with weapons, reaches even shorter distances. Hence, the Alpha Jet and other aircraft like the F-5E, which are shorter-legged vehicles, would be used mainly in the tactical air-to-ground role. They would be most effective in battlefield missions around the Moroccan land-mass, either against the Polisario or against the Spanish enclaves of Ceuta and Melilla, but would be hard-pressed to carry out any "strategic" missions beyond the northwest African promontory. Should Morocco eventually deploy the U.S. F-16—an aircraft it has previously expressed interest in—it would substantially augment its effective long-range strike capability.[4] The F-16 has great combat range: it can carry a wide variety of weapons well into a 500-nm radius, and it could cover the entire Iberian peninsula, under certain flight profiles reaching as far east as the Balearic Islands.

Artillery and battlefield rocket systems. Moroccan artillery and battlefield rocket systems essentially comprise a variety of Russian, American, British, and French systems, all of which are principally effective in battlefield roles.

Table 3 indicates that the maximum effective range of Moroccan artillery is roughly 27 km with standard HE ammunition. Such ranges attainable with the Russian M-46 gun suggest that artillery and battlefield rockets would be most effective when used against targets on

---

[4]The long-run future of the Moroccan air force's F-16 program is uncertain. In November 1991, the U.S. and Moroccan governments agreed to the sale of 20 F-16s, whose delivery schedule was supposed to have been accelerated after the electoral success of the Islamic fundamentalists in Algeria. This program was put on indefinite hold, however, after the Saudi government failed to fund the purchase. To date, no deal has been finalized and no aircraft have been delivered.

the North African landmass, including the Spanish enclaves at Ceuta and Melilla. Theoretically, such artillery could be used for trans-Mediterranean operations, especially if rocket-assisted projectiles and other kinds of extended-range munitions were used; usage in such roles, however, is more academic than practical. Moroccan battlefield MLRS are short-range systems that would be most effective mainly in battlefield operations within the North African continent.

Table 3

Moroccan Artillery and Battlefield Rockets

Weapon System	Type	Caliber	Range	Munitions Capability	Maximum Rate of Fire	Number
British L-118 light gun	Towed	105 mm	17.2 km	HE, HESH, smoke	8 rds/min	35
U.S. M-101	Towed	105 mm	11.2 km	HE, HEAT, smoke, chemical	8 rds/min	20
M-1950	Towed	105 mm				36
Russian M-1946	Towed	130 mm	27 km	HE, APHE	6–7 rds/min	18
U.S. M-114	Towed	155 mm	14.6 km	HE, smoke, illuminating, chemical	2 rds/min	20
FH-70	Towed	155 mm	24 km	HE, smoke, illuminating	6 rds/min	35
U.S. Mk. 52/61	SP	105 mm	11.2 km	HE, HEAT, smoke, chemical, illuminating	3 rds/min	5
French Mk. F3	SP	155 mm	21.6 km	HE, smoke, illuminating	4 rds/min	98
U.S. Mk. 109	SP	155 mm	14.6 km	HE, smoke, illuminating, chemical, nuclear	3 rds/min	44
U.S. Mk. 44	SP	155 mm	14.6 km	HE, smoke, illuminating, chemical	1 rd/min	20
BM-21	MRL: 40 tubes	122 mm	14/20 km	HE, smoke, incendiary, chemical	Reload time: 10 min	39

ALGERIA

WMD Potential or Capabilities

Nuclear facilities. Algeria has two research reactors, ARR-1 and Es SALAM, fully operational. Both are operated by the Haut Commissariat a la Recherche. ARR-1 is a pool-type reactor supplied by Argentina and capable of producing 1 MWe of steady power. It went critical in March 1989. Es SALAM is a heavy-water reactor supplied by China and capable of producing 15 MWe of steady power. It went critical in 1992.[5]

Algeria secretly contracted with China for the construction of the second reactor (SALAM) at Oussera. When the contract was finalized is as yet unknown, but China claims that agreement was reached in February 1983. At any rate, information about the construction was not made public by either Algeria or China, and public knowledge of these developments first came from CIA testimony to Congress in early April 1991. Initially, both Algeria and China denied any collaboration but later acknowledged some details about the reactor under considerable U.S. pressure. The Oussera reactor is capable of producing approximately 3 kg per year of plutonium. The reactor is now under IAEA safeguards, and Algeria will have to accede to comprehensive IAEA inspections, since it is now a signatory to the NPT. The eventual destination of the spent fuel is currently uncertain,[6] though reprocessing at the Draria facility will make it subject to IAEA safeguards.

The history and character of this construction program raise suspicions about Algeria's long-term nuclear intentions. And the Chinese tie could be doubly problematic if it leads to missile sales in the future, as at least one source has speculated.[7]

---

[5] *World Nuclear Industry Handbook 1993*, Surrey, England: Nuclear Engineering International, 1993, p. 120; *Nuclear Research Reactors of the World*, Vienna: IAEA, 1993, p. 30.

[6] The history of the Oussera reactor has been usefully surveyed in Vipin Gupta, "Algeria Nuclear Ambitions," *International Defense Review*, April 1992, pp. 329–331.

[7] "Chinese Nuclear Weapons Reactor for Algeria," *Defence*, May 1991, p. 7.

Algeria has also been identified as an active participant in the underground nuclear trade. In 1987 it had been suspected of transferring uranium dioxide purchased from Argentina for its other research reactors to Iran.[8] More recently, there have been newer allegations that Algeria has accepted about 10 tons of natural uranium smuggled from Iraq and has received technical assistance from Iraqi scientists.[9]

Biological facilities. One source suggests that Algeria has a moderate biological-weapons research capability, probably deriving from its pharmaceutical sector. There are, however, no indications of organized research or of dedicated production facilities.[10]

Chemical facilities. The same source suggests that Algeria possesses the basic technology and industrial infrastructure for producing nerve, mustard, and cyanide gases, again presumably through the state's petrochemical sector. However, no organized chemical warfare research or production facilities are known to exist.[11]

Foreign collaboration and presence. The most significant foreign collaboration with Algeria currently consists of Chinese assistance in the Algerian nuclear program. The number of Chinese personnel in Algeria is not known. Until not too long ago, Algeria was known to have retained between 300 and 500 Russian military advisers. Increasing attacks on foreign residents, including Russians, have probably led to a reduction in this presence.

Delivery Systems

Ballistic missiles. Algeria has no known ballistic missiles in service or in R&D. It is sometimes listed as possessing FROG-7 unguided rockets, but *The Military Balance 1994–95* does not list any FROG systems as operational. At least two sources have speculated, however, about the possibility of future Chinese missile sales to Algeria as

---

[8]Richard Kessler, "Panel to Guide Nuclear Technology Sales from Argentina to Algeria," *Nucleonics Week*, May 7, 1987, p. 6.

[9]"Saddam Helps Algeria Make Islamic Nuclear Bomb," *The Sunday Times*, January 5, 1992.

[10]Cordesman, *Weapons of Mass Destruction*, p. 23.

[11]Ibid.

part of what one analyst calls "China's increasing willingness to play a more proactive role in the region."[12]

Cruise missiles. The Algerian navy deploys one class of short-range surface-to-surface cruise missiles aboard its three *Nanuchka*-class corvettes and eleven *Osa*-class patrol craft, namely the Soviet SS-N-2B Styx. The Nanuchkas and Osas carry four missiles each.

Table 4 indicates that the cruise missiles in the Algerian inventory are essentially short-range tactical weapons designed primarily for anti-surface warfare (ASUW). The Styx missile is interesting because of its relatively large size; it also has a large warhead (513 kg), which makes it a fairly destructive weapon (for its class) and lends itself to warhead modifications of various kinds. Chinese ties with Algeria are particularly significant in this regard because, among other things, China has successfully produced many modifications of the basic Styx design. Should Algeria come to be governed by a radical movement hostile to the West, the desire for such programs or for even newer, more capable acquisitions might take on greater urgency. For the moment, however, Algeria's cruise missile capability rests mainly in short-range patrol boats. Although such boats could harass commercial shipping, especially in the western Mediterranean, they would not survive any encounter with an alerted Western naval flotilla or Western strike aircraft armed with ASMs.

Aircraft. All aircraft capable of strike and ground-attack missions are deployed with the Algerian air force. Algeria traditionally purchased aircraft from the Soviet Union, but more recently it has purchased some Western transport aircraft. Algerian combat aircraft vary in capability from light interceptors with minimal ground-attack capability, like the MiG-21, to highly capable, dedicated strike aircraft like the SU-24 Fencer.

The most capable strike aircraft in the Algerian arsenal is the SU-24 Fencer. Capable of carrying between 4,000 and 8,000 kg of bombs at a distance of about 600 nm, the Fencer can deliver an impressive

---

[12]Gordon Jacobs and Tim McCarthy, "China's Missile Sales: Few Changes for the Future," *Jane's Intelligence Review*, December 1992, p. 563. See also "Chinese Nuclear Weapons Reactor for Algeria," *Defence*, May 1991, p. 7.

Table 4

Algerian Cruise Missiles

Missile	Type	Launch Platform	Number of Platforms	Missile Range (km)	Guidance and Missile Accuracy	Type of Warhead (weight in kg)
SS-N-2B	SSM	Ship	11	46	Autopilot with active radar/IR homing	HE (513)

bomb load on a wide range of targets. If based at Bou-Sfer in north-western Algeria, the Fencer can cover the entire Iberian peninsula, reaching as far east as Toulouse and Marseilles. If based at Biskra in northeastern Algeria, the Fencer can reach well past the western coastline of the Italian peninsula, covering Sicily as well. Lesser capabilities reside in the MiG-23BN, a dedicated ground-attack aircraft capable of ranges in the 300-nm class with full loads. At such ranges, Algeria can target southeastern Spain while covering the entire water basin bounded by Spain and Italy. For the foreseeable future, Algerian attack capabilities will reside primarily in these two classes of aircraft; the fact that both classes could conceivably carry an Algerian nuclear weapon makes further acquisitions of these aircraft a matter of concern.

Artillery and battlefield rocket systems. Algerian artillery and battlefield systems consist exclusively of Russian designs, ranging from the M-1946, with a standard HE shell of 27-km range, to the shorter-range M-1938, which fires a HE shell to about 11 km.

Table 6 suggests that most Algerian artillery systems consist of medium-range weapons—M-1937, D-30, and 2S1—with effective ranges of between 15 and 21 km. Systems capable of delivering ammunitions beyond 20 km are relatively fewer in number (34). There are also several kinds of multiple-launch rocket systems, but all have effective ranges of less than 20 km. On balance, Algerian artillery and rocket systems would be able to affect outcomes mainly on the battlefields of North Africa. They do not have the range to affect southern Europe in the way that the new capabilities of the Algerian air force can.

Table 5

Algerian Combat Aircraft

Aircraft	Primary Mission	Approximate Combat Radius	Approximate Maximum Payload	Types of Weapons Carried	Number
SU-24 Fencer	Dedicated GA	174–565 nm[a]	8,000 kg	General-purpose bombs; rockets; AAMs; ASMs	10
MiG-23 BN	Dedicated GA	378–620 nm[b]	3,000 kg	General-purpose bombs; rockets; AAMs; ASMs	40
MiG-21 MF/bis	Multirole fighter with visual GA capability	200–400 nm[c]	~1,500 kg	AAMs: AA-2; AA-6; 250- and 500-kg bombs and assorted rockets	95 + 3 trainers
MiG-23 M/MS[d]	Interceptor with visual GA capability	485–700 nm	3,000 kg	AAMs	20 + 5 trainers
MiG-25	Dedicated interceptor	675–933 nm		AAMs only	14 + 3 trainers

[a]The 174-nm radius refers to a low-low-low profile. The 565-nm radius refers to a high-low-high profile with 3,000 kg of weapons and two external fuel tanks.

[b]The 378-nm radius presumes the aircraft carries 2,000 kg of bombs. The 620-nm radius is based on an ordnance load of six AAMs.

[c]The 200-nm radius presumes the aircraft to be carrying four 250-kg bombs. The 400-nm radius presumes two 250-kg bombs and external drop tanks.

[d]The MS is the export version of the MiG-23 M. It has a less powerful engine and a less powerful air search radar.

Table 6

Algerian Artillery and Battlefield Rockets

Weapon System	Type	Caliber	Range	Munitions Capability	Max Rate of Fire	Number
Russian D-74	Towed	122 mm	23.9 km	HE, APHE	6–7 rds/min	25
Russian M-1931/37	Towed	122 mm	20.8 km	HE, APHE, smoke	5–6 rds/min	100
Russian M-1938	Towed	122 mm	11.8 km	HE, HEAT, smoke, illuminating	5–6 rds/min	60
Russian D-30	Towed	122 mm	15.3 km	HE, HEAT, smoke, illuminating	7–8 rds/min	190
Russian M-1946	Towed	130 mm	27 km	HE, APHE	6–7 rds/min	10
Russian ML-20	Towed	152 mm	17.3 km	HE, APHE	4 rds/min	20
Russian 2S1	SP	122 mm	15.3 km	HE, HEAT, smoke, illuminating	5–8 rds/min	150
Russian 2S3	SP	152 mm	18.5 km	HE, HEAT, HE/RAP, incendiary, smoke, illuminating, nuclear	4 rds/min	35
Russian BM-21	MRL: 40 tubes	122 mm	14/20 km	HE, smoke, incendiary, chemical	Reload time: 10 min	48
Russian BM-14/16	MRL: 16 tubes	140 mm	10.6 km	HE, smoke, chemical	Reload time: 3–4 min	48
Russian BM-24	MRL: 12 tubes	240 mm	11 km	HE	Reload time: 3–4 min	30

LIBYA

WMD Potential or Capabilities

Nuclear facilities. Libya operates one safeguarded research reactor, IRT-1, at Tajoura. It is a pool-type light-water reactor using highly enriched uranium as fuel and producing 10 MWt of power. It was built by the Soviet Union, which also supplied the enriched fuel under safeguards. It went critical on March 1983.

Libya also has a light-water, low-enriched-uranium power reactor under construction near the Gulf of Sidra. It will be capable of producing 440 MWe, and the reactor and fuel supplied by Russia will be under safeguards.

Libya has no known uranium resources, active mining sites or uranium mills, though it has made some efforts at exploring for uranium.

Libya has had a long history of seeking to acquire nuclear weapons.[13] It attempted to purchase nuclear weapons from China in the 1970s, and after these attempts failed, it developed a network of nuclear trade relations with Pakistan, India, the Soviet Union, Belgium, Argentina, and Brazil. Most of these links atrophied or were terminated by the 1980s, but Libya's commitment to acquiring nuclear weapons has been ongoing. On at least two occasions, Colonel Qadhafi publicly called on the Arab states to acquire nuclear weapons;[14] in 1990, Qadhafi called for the development of Libyan nuclear weapons,[15] a development that is at cross-purposes with Libya's renunciation of nuclear weapons under the NPT.

---

[13]The history of Libyan efforts in the nuclear realm has been well documented in Leonard S. Spector and Jacqueline R. Smith, *Nuclear Ambitions,* Boulder: Westview Press, 1990, pp. 175–185. See also Claudia Wright, "Libya's Nuclear Program," *The Middle East,* February 1982.

[14]"Al-Qadhdhafi Lectures University Students," translated in *FBIS-NES,* June 26, 1987; "Al-Qadhdhafi Discusses Upcoming Amman Summit," translated in *FBIS-NES,* November 3, 1987.

[15]"Al-Qadhdhafi Calls for Arab Nuclear ICBMs," translated in JPRS-TND, April 29, 1990.

Biological facilities. Libya is identified in several sources as having an undeclared offensive biological-weapons program, but the open literature has no information about the extent of Libya's program or biological arsenal, if any.[16] One source suggests that Libya may be trying to acquire the capability to produce limited amounts of biological agents, like anthrax and botulism, in a batch mode but admits that no serious evidence of progress is as yet available.[17] Another source has reported that Libya has a joint biological-warfare program under way in collaboration with Romania.[18]

Chemical facilities.   Libya's chemical-warfare programs are acknowledged by most sources to be the most successful component of its search for WMD. The chemical-weapons production plant at Rabta is understood to be one of the world's largest facilities, with 30 buildings, including two major buildings rarely associated with drug production. The facility also has sheltered underground storage areas and is defended by SAM batteries and ground troops.[19] The Rabta facility is understood to be capable of producing over 1.2 metric tons a day of mustard and nerve gases. It is also designed to produce chemical warheads and munitions, and the dimensions of the physical structure suggest that it was designed to host large loads like missiles. Libya is known to have acquired extensive stocks of key feed stocks like thiodiglycol, required to manufacture mustard gas, as well as large stocks of precursor chemicals required to produce nerve gases. The current operational status of Rabta is uncertain. Libya is known to have had serious startup problems, and the plant appears to have produced only 30–50 tons of mustard gas by March 1990. At that time, Libya claimed that the facility was ravaged by a fire of un-

---

[16]Among the sources that list Libya as having an offensive biological-weapons program is W. Seth Carus, "'The Poor Man's Atomic Bomb?' Biological Weapons in the Middle East," *Policy Papers*, No. 23, Washington, D.C.: The Washington Institute for Near East Policy, 1991; David Fairhall, "Eleven Countries Defying Ban on Germ Weapons," *The Guardian* (London), September 5, 1991; and Elisa Harris, "Towards a Comprehensive Strategy for Halting Chemical and Biological Weapons Proliferation," *Arms Control: Contemporary Security Policy*, Vol. 12, No. 2 (September 1991), p. 29.

[17]Cordesman, *Weapons of Mass Destruction*, pp. 154, 157.

[18]Joseph Douglass, Jr., "Soviets Surge in Biochemical Warfare; West Remains Drugged with Apathy," *Armed Forces Journal International*, August 1988, p. 58.

[19]The most comprehensive description of the Rabta plant can be found in *Focus on Libya*, Washington, D.C.: PEMCON, Ltd., 1990. See also "How Quaddafi Built His Deadly Chemical Plant," *Business Week*, January 23, 1989.

known origin, though the extent of the damage claimed was probably exaggerated.   One British official is quoted as claiming that "the burning down of the Rabta plant ... was just a show with rubber tyres."[20]

In addition to the Rabta plant, Libya also has a small pilot facility located near Tripoli that began production in late 1987 and appears to be the main source of its poison gas stockpile. There have also been rumors of a second major chemical facility under construction at Sabha, 460 miles south of Tripoli, with Chinese assistance.[21]

Libya's chemical production capabilities have been assisted by several international suppliers, including European and Japanese firms. The Rabta plant was constructed in great measure with assistance from West German firms, particularly Imhausenchemie AG. The pilot plant outside Tripoli is said to be operated by the North Koreans with some support from Iranian technicians, who are supposed to have also modified Libyan Scud missiles to carry chemical warheads.[22]

Libya has used chemical weapons in war, most notably in Chad during 1986–1987. It has been suggested that the mustard gas used in this conflict was acquired from Iran in exchange for Soviet-made mines or Scud-B missiles.[23]

Foreign collaboration and presence.   Following the embargo on Libya, most open foreign collaboration with Libya ceased. However, 300–500 foreign advisers are still known to be serving under individual contracts. The nationality of these advisers is not known, but they are suspected to be from North Korea, Russia, Iran, Syria, and West Germany.

---

[20]Holly Porteous, "Ridding Iraq of CW to Take Two Years," *Jane's Defence Weekly*, September 28, 1991, p. 557.

[21]Cordesman, *Weapons of Mass Destruction*, pp. 153–157. Since this research was completed, the United States has publicly confirmed the existence of a new chemical-weapons production facility at Tarkunah. This facility, suspected to be the world's largest underground chemical-weapons plant, is expected to be operational by the end of this decade.

[22]Ibid.

[23]"The Year in Missiles," *Defense and Foreign Affairs*, March 1988, p. 22.

Delivery Systems

Ballistic missiles. Libya's ballistic missile arsenal currently consists of Scud missiles and FROG-7 rockets.

Libyan ballistic missile capabilities, currently dependent on the Scud-B and FROG-7 rockets, provide a tactical strike capability that can threaten substantial areas of Libya's regional neighbors, Egypt, Chad, Niger and Algeria, as well as the offshore islands in the Mediterranean. Libyan ballistic missiles currently cannot threaten the mainland of southern Europe, unless they are based in Tunisia. Scud-Bs based in Tunisia will allow Libya to target parts of Sardinia and Sicily. Libya is believed to have at least three times as many missiles as it has missile launchers.[24] In 1986 Libya fired two Scuds at the U.S. Coast Guard facility at Lampedusa, off the Italian coast.

Libya's lack of strategic reach has precipitated a search for more sophisticated weapon systems. On several occasions, Libya has tried to purchase longer-range missiles, including the Russian SS-12 and the

Table 7

Libyan Ballistic Missiles

Missile	Mobility	Guidance System	Accuracy (CEP in m)	Range (km)	Type of Warhead (weight in kg)	Number of Launchers
FROG-7	Mobile	Unguided	500	70	HE, chemical [?] (435)	40
Scud-B	Mobile	Inertial	900–1,000	300	HE, chemical[a] (985)	80
Al Fatah[b] (under development)				950 [?]	500 [?]	

[a]Anthony Cordesman cites reports suggesting that some Libyan Scuds have been armed with chemical warheads. Cordesman, *Weapons of Mass Destruction in the Middle East,* London: Brasseys, 1991, p. 154.

[b]Duncan Lennox, "Missile Race Continues," *Jane's Defence Weekly,* January 23, 1993, p. 18.

---

[24]S. Zaloga, "Ballistic Missiles in the Third World: Scud and Beyond," *International Defense Review,* November 1988, pp. 1423–1427.

Chinese CSS-2.[25] Libya has also attempted to acquire ballistic missiles from Brazil; has financed a West German firm, Otrag, to produce a rocket in the 300–500-km range; and in recent years is rumored to have linked up with the North Koreans in an attempt to acquire the 1,000-km-range Scud-D (or perhaps the Nodong-1) missile.[26]

Of more troubling significance is the Libyan effort to construct a 950-km liquid-propelled missile dubbed "Al Fatah." This missile program, currently under development with German, Brazilian, or Chinese participation, was presumed dead until a report in May 1990 suggested that the program was under way and that static motor tests could be expected in the future.[27] The Al Fatah, when operational, would result in a significant extension of Libyan missile reach. Missiles like the Al-Fatah or the North Korean Scud-D, if based near Tripoli, would allow Libya to target Sardinia, Sicily, and southern Italy, including Rome. If based near Tobruk, Libyan missiles could threaten Greece, western Turkey, and almost all of Egypt. If these missiles were deployed in Tunisia, Libya could target almost all of Italy, southeast France, and eastern Spain.

The Libyan attempts to acquire or develop long-range ballistic missiles, especially those with unconventional warheads, will remain a matter of serious concern in the coming decade. Particular attention will have to be focused on Libyan arrangements with China, North Korea, and Syria in this regard.

Cruise missiles. Libya's cruise missiles are based principally on board its naval vessels and consist mainly of the Soviet Styx, the Otomat SSM, and the French SS-12M. The missile-carrying naval

---

[25]"Libya is developing SSM," *Flight International*, May 23, 1987, p. 10.

[26]"Libya: Defense Organization/Strength," Periscope database, June 17, 1992. The North Korean "Scud-D" is different from the Soviet Scud-D. The North Korean version is a 1,000-km-range weapon with a CEP of about 750 meters. The Soviet version is a 300-km-range weapon with a 50-meter CEP attained probably through the use of a terminal seeker. See Joseph Bermudez, "Ballistic Ambitions Ascendant," *Jane's Defence Weekly*, April 10, 1993, pp. 20–22; "SS-1 Scud," *Jane's Strategic Weapons Systems*, Issue 10; Paul Beaver, "Nodong-1 Details Fuel New Fears in Asia," *Jane's Defence Weekly*, January 15, 1994, p. 4.

[27]"Unclassified Projects: Offensive Systems," *Jane's Strategic Weapons Systems*, Issue 12.

Table 8

Libyan Cruise Missiles

Missile	Type	Launch Platform	Number of Platforms	Missile Range (km)	Guidance and Missile Accuracy	Type of Warhead (weight in kg)
SS-N-2C Styx	SSM	Ship	17	83	Autopilot with active radar/IR homing	HE (513)
Otomat Mk. 2	SSM	Ship	14	180	Inertial with command update and active radar	HE, semiarmor piercing (210)
SS-12M	SSM	Ship	3	5.5	Wire-guided	HE (30)
AM-39	ASM	Helicopter	5	50	Inertial with active radar	HE, shaped charge fragmentation (165)

order of battle consists of one UK *Vosper*-class frigate with four Otomat Mk. 2; two Soviet *Koni*-class frigates with four SS-N-2C Styx each; three Soviet *Nanuchka*- and twelve Soviet *Osa II*-class patrol boats with four SS-N-2C Styx each; four *Assad*-class corvettes (three are believed to be nonoperational) and nine French *Combattante II*-class missile craft with four Otomat Mk. 2 each; and three *Susa*-class missile craft with eight French SS-12M each. In addition, Libya has fifteen SA321 Super Frelon ASW helicopters armed with the AM-39 Exocet ASM.

The longest-range antiship cruise missile in the Libyan arsenal is the Otomat Mk. 2, with a range of 180 km. For this range to be effective, however, the missile requires midcourse updating information supplied either by aircraft or helicopter. All other missiles have shorter maximum ranges, though the Soviet Styx has a substantially larger warhead. Modifying either the warhead or the guidance packages to give antiship cruise missiles a land-attack orientation is presently outside of Libyan technical capabilities, though this task might be accomplished if international assistance is forthcoming.

Given Libya's conspicuous lack of accomplishment in the area of high technology, it is unlikely that a Libyan WMD would be delivered by cruise missile. The more prominent candidates here are delivery by aircraft and ballistic missiles or by more unconventional methods, such as terrorism.

Aircraft. All aircraft capable of strike and ground-attack missions are deployed with the Libyan air force, which is large and predominantly Soviet equipped, though with some significant French equipment. The strike component is particularly conspicuous and consists of MiG-23BNs, Mirage Vs, SU-22s, and most capable of all, the Soviet SU-24 Fencer.

The large numbers of fairly sophisticated aircraft bequeath to the Libyan air force a considerable capability to deliver WMD. This fact must be qualified, however, by the recognition that maintenance of Libyan aircraft is usually poor and Libya often depends on foreign pilots and instructors to supply it with the personnel it needs to man its air force.

The most capable Libyan strike aircraft is the SU-24, with a combat radius in the 600-nm class; this range allows it to reach southern Italy, Greece, and western Turkey. Under certain flight profiles, it could conceivably even reach Israel. Libya also has a small contingent of TU-22 bombers, whose effective combat radius and payload are even greater than that of the SU-24. These aircraft, however, are for most practical purposes obsolete and could not penetrate any alerted air defense system.

Less capable systems include the Mirage F-1 in various versions, followed closely by the Russian MiG-23BN and the French Mirage 5. Taken together, these aircraft comprise a force of over 100 aircraft capable of carrying ordnance to a range of 300–400 nm. Such reach enables Libya to deliver at least large numbers of chemical weapons to various parts of the North African continent, the offshore islands in the Mediterranean, Greece, and perhaps even Turkey.

Other Libyan aircraft like the SU-20/22 and the MiG-21 bis are short-legged aircraft that would be restricted to operations in North Africa.

Table 9

Libyan Combat Aircraft

Aircraft	Primary Mission	Approximate Combat Radius	Approximate Maximum Payload	Types of Weapons Carried	Number
TU-22	Bomber	700–1,185 nm	12,000 kg	General-purpose bombs; ASMs	6 + 1 trainer
MiG-23 BN	Dedicated GA	378–620 nm[a]	3,000 kg	General-purpose bombs; rockets; AAMs, ASMs	40 + 15 trainers
Mirage 5D/DE, DD	Dedicated GA	350–700 nm[b]	4,000 kg	General-purpose bombs; rockets; AAMs, ASMs	44
Mirage F-1BD/ED	Dedicated GA	230–750 nm[c]	6,500 kg	General-purpose bombs; rockets; AAMs, ASMs	18
Mirage F-1AD	Interceptor with visual GA capability	230–750 nm[c]	6,500 kg	General-purpose bombs; rockets; AAMs, ASMs	14
SU-24 Fencer	Dedicated GA	174–565 nm[d]	8,000 kg	General-purpose bombs; rockets; AAMs, ASMs	6
SU-20/22	Dedicated GA	240–370 nm[e]	4,250 kg	General-purpose bombs; rockets; AAMs, ASMs	45
MiG-21 bis	Multirole fighter with visual GA capability	200–400 nm[f]	~1,500 kg	AAMs: AA-2, AA-6; 250- and 500-kg bombs and assorted rockets	50
MiG-23 MF	Interceptor with visual GA capability	328–620 nm[a]	3,000 kg	AAMs; bombs	75
MiG-25	Dedicated interceptor	675–933 nm		AAMs only	60 + 3 trainers

[a]The 378-nm radius presumes the aircraft carries 2,000 kg of bombs. The 620-nm radius is based on an ordnance load of six AAMs.

[b]The 350-nm radius presumes a 907-kg bomb load and a low-low-low profile. The 700-nm figure presumes a high-low-high profile with the same load.

[c]The 230-nm radius presumes a high-low-high profile with a 3,500-kg bomb load. The 750-nm radius presumes a high-low-high profile with a 500-kg bomb load and three external tanks. If a low-low-low profile is considered with a bomb load of about 1,500 kg and two external tanks, the combat radius of the Mirage F-1 is roughly 325 nm.

[d]The 174-nm radius refers to a low-low-low profile. The 565-nm radius refers to a high-low-high profile with 3,000 kg of weapons and two external fuel tanks.

[e]The 240-nm radius presumes the aircraft to be carrying a 2,000-kg bomb load with external fuel and flying a low-low-low profile. The 370-nm radius presumes the same loads but a high-low-high profile.

[f]The 200-nm radius presumes the aircraft to be carrying four 250-kg bombs. The 400-nm radius presumes two 250-kg bombs and external drop tanks.

Among the more troubling developments with respect to Libyan aviation has been the reported acquisition of a Russian IL-28 tanker aircraft.[28] The presence of such an aircraft extends the reach of both Libyan bombers and its other strike aircraft, allowing them to reach a perimeter even wider than that identified above. With refueling capabilities, Libya can actually reach important population centers in the southern European region. Libya has had an interest in air-to-air refueling capabilities for many years and is known to have experimentally refueled a Mirage F-1 from a C-130 aircraft configured for the tanker role by a West German company.[29] The continued desire for, and presence of, dedicated Libyan refueling aircraft only signifies greater increases in Libya's future reach.

Artillery and battlefield rocket systems. Libyan artillery and rocket systems consist of predominantly Russian equipment with some American and Italian equipment as well.

The longest-range artillery system, the Soviet M-1946 with a standard range of 27 km, is also the system deployed in largest numbers. All other systems have shorter range, and Libyan artillery capabilities taken together suggest only normal battlefield reach. Libya has a large collection of Russian BM-21 multiple rocket launchers (600), but with ranges not exceeding 20 km, these systems too will be effective only against North African adversaries rather than the Mediterranean states lying offshore.

---

[28]"Libya: Air Force," Periscope database, June 17, 1992.

[29]William Tuohy, "W. German Firm Helping Libya in Refueling Project, Magazine Says," *Philadelphia Inquirer*, January 16, 1989.

Table 10

Libyan Artillery and Battlefield Rockets

Weapon System	Type	Caliber	Range	Munitions Capability	Max Rate of Fire	Number
U.S. M-101	Towed	105 mm	11.2 km	HE, HEAT, smoke, chemical	8 rds/min	60
Russian D-30	Towed	122 mm	15.3 km	HE, HEAT, smoke, illuminating	7–8 rds/min	270
Russian D-74	Towed	122 mm	23.9 km	HE, APHE	6–7 rds/min	60
Russian M-1946	Towed	130 mm	27 km	HE, APHE	6–7 rds/min	330
Russian 2S1	SP	122 mm	15.3 km	HE, HEAT, smoke, illuminating	5–8 rds/min	130
Russian 2S3	SP	152 mm	18.5 km	HE, HEAT, HE/RAP, incendiary, smoke, illuminating, nuclear	4 rds/min	40
Italian Palmaria	SP	155 mm	24 km	HE, HE/RAP, smoke, illuminating	4 rds/min	160
U.S. Mk. 109	SP	155 mm	14.6 km	HE, smoke, illuminating, chemical, nuclear	3 rds/min	20
Chinese Type 63	MRL: 12 tubes	107 mm	8.3 km	HE, HE-incendiary, HE-frag		700
Russian BM-21	MRL: 40 tubes	122 mm	14/20 km	HE, smoke, incendiary, chemical	Reload time: 10 min	Included in above total
Russian RM-70	MRL: 40 tubes	122 mm	20.3 km	HE, smoke, chemical	Reload time: 3–4 min	Included in above total
Russian BM-11		122 mm				Included in above total

EGYPT

WMD Potential or Capabilities

Nuclear facilities. Egypt has one research reactor, ETRR-1, producing 2 MWt of steady power. It is a tank-type reactor operated by the Egyptian Atomic Energy Authority, and it went critical in February 1961. A second research reactor built to a similar design, ETRR-2, is planned. It is intended to produce 20 MWt of steady power.

Egypt also plans to construct two power reactors at El Dabaa near Alexandria. These reactors are designed for a licensed production of 1,000 MWe each. To date, no information is available about planned construction and completion dates.[30] Egypt is not known to have any nuclear fuel cycle facilities.

Egypt is not known currently to have any active nuclear weapons research program, though some interest was evinced after the 1956 conflict over Suez. This interest quickly dissipated in favor of chemical and biological weapons research. All current nuclear research appears to be a continuation of the basic research begun in 1961 and is generally acknowledged to be a low-level research effort.[31]

Biological facilities. Egypt is not usually identified as having an undeclared offensive biological-weapons program, but some sources have raised questions in this regard.[32] One suggests that Egypt has not only the requisite laboratory and technical base but "could go rapidly into [biological weapons] production."[33] This lab and technical base is presumably shared by the country's pharmaceutical industry, but no other information about the character of Egypt's biological-weapons program is available in the open literature.

---

[30] *World Nuclear Industry Handbook 1993*, pp. 28–29, 121.

[31] Cordesman, *Weapons of Mass Destruction*, p. 25.

[32] Among the sources that do list Egypt as having a biological-weapons program are David Fairhall, "Eleven Countries"; a Russian Federation Foreign Intelligence Service Report titled "A New Challenge After the Cold War: Proliferation of Weapons of Mass Destruction," reprinted in JPRS-TND-93-007; and the U.S. Arms Control and Disarmament Agency, "Adherence to and Compliance with Arms Control Agreements and The President's Report to Congress on Soviet Noncompliance with Arms Control," Washington, D.C.: ACDA, January 14, 1993.

[33] Cordesman, *Weapons of Mass Destruction*, p. 143.

Chemical facilities. Egypt's chemical-warfare programs are considered to be the most extensive of its research programs dealing with weapons of mass destruction. Egypt was known to have the capability to produce mustard gas since the early 1960s, and mustard gas was used operationally against the Royalists in the Yemeni civil war. During the 1973 war with Israel, large quantities of defensive chemical weapons gear were captured, although possessing such gear may simply have been a function of following Soviet operating procedures. Egypt's ability to manufacture mustard gas—a capability flowing easily from the possession of a petrochemical industry—is generally acknowledged by most sources, but whether it can manufacture persistent and nonpersistent nerve gases—which require specialized and perhaps dedicated facilities—is still somewhat uncertain. One source, alluding to Israeli intelligence, indicates that Egypt is constructing chemical-weapons feed stock plants north of Cairo.[34] These facilities would presumably enable Egypt to produce nerve gases without dependence on imports for precursor chemicals.

Egyptian chemical weapons are generally asserted to take the form of bombs and shells, but it is uncertain whether Egypt has chemical warheads for its Scud and FROG missiles. Such warheads, however, would not be difficult to manufacture. The Egyptian chemical-weapons program is significant, though it is not as large as comparable programs in Libya, Syria, and Iraq.

Foreign collaboration and presence. The most significant foreign collaboration with Egypt consists of North Korean assistance in Egypt's ballistic missile program. The number of North Koreans, if any, in Egypt is unknown. Egypt also has instructors from France and the United States currently serving on deputation, and foreign trainees from several African and Middle Eastern states.

Delivery Systems

Ballistic missiles. Egypt's ballistic missile arsenal currently consists of Scud missiles and FROG-7 rockets as well as a new indigenously developed unguided rocket system, the SAKR-80. This system has

---

[34]Ibid.

Table 11

Egyptian Ballistic Missiles

Missile	Mobility	Guidance System	Accuracy (CEP in m)	Range (km)	Type of Warhead (weight in kg)	Number of Launchers
FROG-7	Mobile	Unguided	500	70	HE, chemical [?] (435)	12
Scud-B	Mobile	Inertial	900–1,000	300	HE, chemical [?] (985)	9

been developed as a replacement for the FROG-7, and is listed in the section on battlefield artillery and rockets.

Egypt's Scud-B missiles are in general rather short-legged weapons that at present allow it to target only Israel, portions of eastern Libya, and, if deployed to the south, northern Sudan. Both the original Scuds and FROGs acquired in the early 1970s are now obsolete, so Egypt has made concentrated efforts to upgrade its missile inventory with longer-range systems. Since the early 1980s, Egypt has collaborated with North Korea to produce a longer-range variant of the Scud-B.[35] This program, sometimes identified as "Project T," is supposed to produce a missile of 450-km range (one and a half times that of the Scud) while carrying the same Scud-sized warhead (985 kg).[36] Whether production of these weapons has begun is unclear, but at least one source suggests that production began in 1990 and that a 90-missile inventory is planned.[37] Whether or not this information is accurate, it must be expected that Egypt will acquire enhanced-range Scud variants in the coming years. The North Korean connection is most promising in this regard, and it has been speculated that Egypt could acquire either the North Korean Scud-C

---

[35]Robert D. Sheuy et al., *Missile Proliferation: Survey of Emerging Missile Forces*, Washington, D.C.: Congressional Research Service, February 9, 1989, p. 45. A detailed analysis of the Egyptian missile program can also be found in Joseph S. Bermudez, Jr., "Ballistic Missile Development in Egypt," *Jane's Intelligence Review*, October 1992, pp. 452–458.

[36]"Unclassified Projects: Offensive Weapons," *Jane's Weapons Systems*, Issue 12.

[37]Ibid.

(600-km range) or even the Scud-D (1,000-km range).[38] Missiles in this class would extend Egypt's targeting reach substantially: the former would allow Egypt to reach well beyond Crete to the southern Greek islands, portions of southern Turkey, Cyprus, and, in the northeast, well into western Syria; the latter would allow Egypt to target almost all of Greece, almost all of Turkey, and reach well into western Iraq and northwestern Saudi Arabia.

Besides work on the Scud variants, Egypt has also explored other missile development programs. Egypt and Argentina were actively involved in a joint R&D effort aimed at producing the Condor II missile, sometimes known as the Badr-2000. This program also involved Iraqi collaboration and was intended to produce a missile of 1,200-km range carrying a payload of 450 kg. This collaboration has now been terminated, but Egypt continues to attempt autonomous development of a missile in the 1,000-km class, occasionally identified by the codename Vector. It is not known if any Condor technologies have been transferred to support this effort, but it must be noted that the Condor program was terminated before any flight testing took place. A missile of this class would allow Egypt to reach small portions of Sicily and southern Italy in the west, as far as Bulgaria in the north, almost two-thirds of Iraq in the northeast, and substantial portions of Saudi Arabia in the southeast.

Cruise missiles. Egyptian cruise missiles are based principally on board its naval vessels, though helicopter-carried missiles and shore-based batteries also exist. The Egyptian cruise missile inventory consists of the Soviet Styx; the Chinese version of the Styx, the CSS-N-2; the Italian Otomat Mk. 2; and the U.S. Harpoon. The missile-carrying naval order of battle consists of two Spanish *Descubierta-*class frigates, each carrying 2 × 4 Harpoon SSMs; two Chinese Jianghu I frigates, each with two CSS-N-2 SSMs; six *Ramadan-*class missile craft, each with four Otomat Mk. 1 SSMs; six Soviet *Osa-*class missile boats, each with four SS-N-2A Styx SSMs; six *October 6th-*class missile boats, each with two Otomat Mk. 1 SSMs; six Chinese Hegu missile craft (Russian *Komar-*class), each with two CSS-N-2 SSMs; and two ex-Soviet *Komar-*class boats with two SS-N-2A Styx SSMs. The Otomat and the Styx also exist in coastal defense batter-

---

[38]Bermudez, "Ballistic Missile Development in Egypt," p. 454.

ies, and the helicopter-carried antisurface weapon appears to be the AM-39 Exocet. One Chinese *Romeo*-class submarine is also reported to be equipped with sub-launched Harpoon, and another three boats are currently undergoing modernization.

Table 12 indicates that Egyptian cruise missiles are exclusively anti-shipping cruise missiles with ranges varying from 50 km, as in the case of the helicopter-launched Exocet, to about 130 km, in the case of the Harpoon. With the exception of the Harpoon carried aboard the *Descubierta*-class frigates and the *Romeo*-class submarine, all

Table 12

Egyptian Cruise Missiles

Missile	Type	Launch Platform	Number of Platforms	Missile Range (km)	Guidance and Missile Accuracy	Type of Warhead (weight in kg)
SS-N-2A Styx	SSM	Ship	8	46	Autopilot with active radar/IR homing	HE (513)
CSS-N-2 (Chinese SS-N-2C Styx variant)	SSM	Ship	8	85	Autopilot with active radar/IR homing	HE (400)
Otomat Mk. 1	SSM	Ship	12	80	Inertial with command update and active radar	HE, semiarmor piercing (210)
Otomat coastal defense system[a]	SSM	Shore battery	3 batteries	6–100	Inertial with command update and active radar	HE, semiarmor piercing (210)
Harpoon	SSM SubSM	Ship/ submarine	3	130	Inertial with active radar	HE (227)
AM-39	ASM	Helicopter	12	50	Inertial with active radar	HE shaped charge frag-mentation (165)

[a]Includes three Sea King Mk. 47 helicopters fitted for target updating so that missiles can be used to maximum range.

other shipborne missiles are carried aboard small brown-water-capable missile craft. After Israel, Egypt has the second-largest technical infrastructure in the Middle East; consequently, if missile modifications are desired, Egypt is advantageously positioned to undertake them. For the foreseeable future, however, should Egypt desire to develop delivery systems for its WMD, aircraft followed by ballistic missiles would be its systems of choice. This is particularly so because, after Israel, Egypt possesses the best-equipped and best-trained air force in the Middle East.

In addition to dedicated cruise missiles, Egypt is known to possess a large number of remotely piloted vehicles (RPVs), at least some of which are armed. Egypt has at least one armed multirole RPV, but at the moment such weapons appear designed primarily for battlefield use rather than for strategic land attack.[39] Given that the basic technology has been perfected, there is no reason why such RPVs cannot be developed into dedicated strategic land attack weapons in the future. The chief of operations of the Egyptian air force has already intimated that Egypt is planning a large-scale expansion of RPV roles, including those involved in combat.[40]

Aircraft. All aircraft capable of strike and ground-attack missions are deployed with the Egyptian air force, which, after several decades of exclusively using Soviet equipment, is now in the midst of completing its transition to Western aircraft. As a result, both older-generation Soviet aircraft like the MiG-21 and highly modern Western aircraft like the U.S. F-16 and the French Mirage 2000 coexist in the arsenal. The large Egyptian air force is predominantly oriented to air defense missions, and its dedicated strike component, consisting primarily of the U.S. F-4 Phantom and the French Mirage 5, is small in comparison.

The U.S. F-4E Phantom and the French Mirage 5 constitute the dedicated strike capabilities of the Egyptian air force. The Phantom can carry over 5,000 kg of payload, and both Phantom and Mirage can

---

[39]Robert Salvy and Jacques Clostermann, "Strength in Diversity," *International Defense Review*, January 1990, p. 64.
[40]Ibid.

Table 13

Egyptian Combat Aircraft

Aircraft	Primary Mission	Approximate Combat Radius	Approximate Maximum Payload	Types of Weapons Carried	Number
Alpha Jet	Light attack/COIN aircraft	340–580 nm	2,500 kg	Mixed fuel, bomb and rocket loads; under-fuselage podded cannon	40
J-6	Light attack	370 nm[a]	~1,000 kg	Mixed fuel, bomb and rocket loads	40 + 16 trainers
Mirage 5E2	Dedicated GA	350–700 nm[b]	4,000 kg	General-purpose bombs; rockets; AAMs; ASMs	16
F-4E	Multirole fighter with automated GA capability	600 nm	7,250 kg	General-purpose bombs; rockets; AAMs; ASMs	25
F-16A	Multirole fighter with automated GA capability	>500 nm	5,400 kg	General-purpose bombs; rockets; AAMs; ASMs	30 + 15 trainers
F-16C	Multirole fighter with automated GA capability	340–740 nm[c]	5,400 kg	General-purpose bombs; rockets; AAMs; ASMs	80 + 6 trainers
Mirage 5D/E,	Dedicated GA	350–700 nm[b]	4,000 kg	General-purpose bombs; rockets; AAMs; ASMs	54 + 5 trainers
Mirage 2000	Multirole fighter with automated GA capability	500–650 nm	6,000 kg	General-purpose bombs; rockets; AAMs; ASMs	16 + 3 trainers
J-7	Multirole fighter with visual GA capability	200–324 nm	~1,500 kg	General-purpose bombs; rockets; AAMs	60
MiG-21 MF	Multirole fighter with visual GA capability	200–400 nm[d]	~1,500 kg	AAMs; 250- and 500-kg bombs and assorted rockets	100 + some trainers

[a]Assumes 800-liter external tanks and air-to-air weapons only.
[b]The 350-nm radius presumes a 907-kg bomb load and a low-low-low profile. The 700-nm figure presumes a high-low-high profile with the same load.
[c]The 340-nm radius presumes an approximately 4,000-kg bomb load, two Sidewinder AAMs, 1,136 liters of external fuel, and a high-low-high profile. The 740-nm radius presumes an approximately 2,000-kg bomb load, three Sidewinders, 3,940 liters of external fuel, and the same flight profile.
[d]The 200-nm radius presumes the aircraft to be carrying four 250-kg bombs. The 400-nm radius presumes two 250-kg bombs and external drop tanks.

operate well into the 400-nm range; this enables coverage of most of the eastern Mediterranean, including parts of Greece and Turkey.

The Mirage 2000 and the F-16 can also carry 5,000-kg loads over slightly longer ranges, and both have automated ground-attack capabilities, but both aircraft are currently used predominantly in the air intercept role. All of Egypt's other aircraft, like the J-7, J-6, and MiG-21, are short-legged aircraft with effective ranges in the 200-nm class, and thus they are more useful for CAS/BAI than for deep strike missions.

The Egyptian air force has continued priority in defense allocations, and future acquisitions will consist of further purchases of F-16 and Mirage 2000 aircraft. The quality of the Egyptian air force itself will progressively increase as all the older Soviet-supplied aircraft of the 1970s are phased out of service. If the additional F-16s and Mirage 2000s envisaged for the future are deployed in the ground-attack role, the effective strike capabilities of the Egyptian air force as a whole will also progressively extend.

Artillery and battlefield rocket systems. Egyptian artillery systems consist primarily of Soviet equipment acquired during the pre-1973 period. In recent years, this equipment has been supplemented by some U.S. equipment, primarily self-propelled artillery, and by indigenous systems, primarily multiple launch battlefield rocket systems.

Table 14 indicates that the largest single system (M-1946: 420 pieces) in the inventory also happens to be the longest-range artillery system (27 km) in Egyptian service. All other systems have smaller standard ranges. Egyptian tube artillery would be most efficacious in battlefield operations, and its ranges in the 11–27 km class essentially enable Egypt to deliver ordnance on the North African landmass rather than across the Mediterranean.

Egypt's indigenously designed MLRS, the SAKR series, is much longer ranged in comparison to the country's tube artillery. The most capable system, the SAKR-80, was designed as a replacement for the FROG-7; unlike the FROG, however, which is configured at one missile to a launcher, the SAKR-80 consists of 3 or 4 missiles carried on a single mobile launcher. Capable of reaching a range of 80 km, the SAKR-80 provides a powerful, longer-range, mobile com-

Table 14

Egyptian Artillery and Battlefield Rockets

Weapon System	Type	Caliber	Range	Munitions Capability	Maximum Rate of Fire	Number
Russian M-1931/37	Towed	122 mm	20.8 km	HE, APHE, smoke	5–6 rds/min	36
Russian M-1938	Towed	122 mm	11.8 km	HE, HEAT, smoke, illuminating	5–6 rds/min	359
Russian D-30	Towed	122 mm	15.3 km	HE, HEAT, smoke, illuminating	7–8 rds/min	156
Russian M-1946	Towed	130 mm	27 km	HE, APHE	6–7 rds/min	420
U.S. Mk. 109A2	SP	155 mm	14.6 km	HE, smoke, illuminating, chemical, nuclear	3 rds/min	200
Russian BM-11	MRL: 40 tubes	122 mm				96
Russian BM-21	MRL: 40 tubes	122 mm	14/20 km	HE, smoke, incendiary, chemical	Reload time: 10 min	200
SAKR-36	MRL: 40-, 30-, and 21-tube versions	122 mm	36 km	HE, HE-frag, Submunitions including antipersonnel and antitank minelaying		Included in above total
SAKR-18	MRL: 40-, 30-, and 21-tube versions	122 mm	18–20 km	Submunitions including antipersonnel and antitank minelaying		Included in above total
SAKR-10	MRL: 1-, 3-, 4-, and 8-tube versions	122 mm	3–10.8 km	HE, HE-frag		Included in above total
SAKR-80	MRL: 3- or 4-tube launcher	325 mm	80 km	HE-frag, ICM, HE-shaped charge, with a 200-kg warhead weight		In service; number N/A

plement to Egypt's tube artillery. It extends the range of Egypt's battlefield reach, but its effects will be felt only in the North African arena. The SAKR series presently is designed to carry conventional explosives and submunitions designed for antipersonnel and antitank missions, but there is no reason in principle why it cannot be equipped with chemical warheads if Egypt so chooses. There have been reports that Egypt has increased its collaboration with China, with the intention of improving its SSMs and battlefield rocket systems as well as acquiring new antiship cruise missiles. This development could be increasingly significant in the future.

SYRIA

WMD Potential or Capabilities

Nuclear facilities. Syria is not considered to have any serious nuclear aspirations. A pool-type nuclear research reactor capable of producing 10 MWt of steady power has apparently been planned, but as yet no evidence of construction is available.[41] In the 1980s, Syria announced ambitious nuclear energy plans that included the construction of as many as six nuclear power reactors capable of producing 6,000 MW of power; all these plans have now been indefinitely shelved.[42]

In the past, Syria had also approached the Soviet Union, Italy, China, and Argentina for nuclear reactors, and in 1991 it bought from China a miniature 30-kW neutron source reactor, together with 980.4 grams of highly enriched uranium. This facility is reportedly not suitable for making nuclear weapons.[43]

Syria has no known uranium resources and is not known to have any fuel cycle facilities.

Biological facilities. Syria is known to be interested in offensive biological warfare and has been identified by at least six sources as hav-

---

[41] *World Nuclear Industry Handbook, 1993,* p. 123.

[42] Michael Eisenstadt, "Syria's Strategic Weapons," *Jane's Intelligence Review,* April 1993, p. 169.

[43] Ibid.

ing an ongoing biological warfare program.[44] One source, in fact, identifies Syria as possessing "at least one major biological warfare facility, and possibly two";[45] it asserts, further, that Syria is known to have an extensive research effort and has possibly produced botulism as well as other agents.[46]

Chemical facilities. Syria's chemical-warfare programs are generally understood to be the most successful component of its unconventional weapons program. Syrian chemical-weapons efforts began in earnest after the 1982 clash with Israel, and since then they have focused principally on the production of nerve gases and on modification of the weapons intended to deliver them. It is suggested that Syria operates two and possibly three facilities for producing chemical weapons near Damascus and Homs.[47] One source indicates that the Damascus facility produces mustard gas and Sarin, with VX possibly under development.[48]

Syrian chemicals are carried principally by air-delivered bombs: Nerve agents like VX and Sarin apparently arm various air-delivered bombs, and it has been suggested that the Soviet ZAB-series incendiary bomb and the PTAB-500 cluster bomb series have been modified to carry chemical agents.[49] However, chemical warheads delivered through artillery tubes and MRL have also been mentioned, and blister agents like mustard gas are mentioned as the agent. Syria also has chemical warheads for its Scud missiles: the Soviet chemical warhead for this system has received wide publicity, and the design has been widely available in the Third World since the 1970s. It has been stated that West European and North Korean engineers have

---

[44]Among the sources that list Syria as having an offensive biological-weapons program are W. Seth Carus, "The Poor Man's Atomic Bomb?"; Fairhall, "Eleven Countries"; Harris, "Towards a Comprehensive Strategy," p. 129; U.S. Arms Control and Disarmament Agency, "Adherence to and Compliance with Arms Control Agreements"; Cordesman, *Weapons of Mass Destruction*, p. 145; and Eisenstadt, "Syria's Strategic Weapons," p. 169.

[45]Cordesman, *Weapons of Mass Destruction*, p. 145.

[46]Ibid., p. 28.

[47]Ibid., p. 27.

[48]Andrew Rathmell, "Chemical Weapons in the Middle East: Syria, Iran, Iraq and Libya," *Marine Corps Gazette*, July 1990, p. 62.

[49]Cordesman, *Weapons of Mass Destruction*, p. 146.

played prominent roles in arming Syria's Scuds, but there is some dispute about whether Syrian SS-21s have been armed with chemical warheads.[50]

Foreign collaboration and presence. The most significant foreign collaboration with Syria currently consists of North Korean assistance in the Syrian ballistic missile program. The number of North Korean personnel, if any, in Syria is not known. Syria is known to have, however, about 500 Russian military advisers, mainly in air defense. Advisers from Bulgaria, Hungary, and China are also reported.

Delivery Systems

Ballistic missiles. Syria's ballistic missile arsenal currently consists of Scud and SS-21 missiles and FROG-7 rockets.

Syria considers its ballistic missile force an important component of its arsenal. The ballistic missile brigades of the Syrian army have elevated importance because of the Syrian air force's demonstrated inability to successfully penetrate Israeli air space. The longest-range missile in the current inventory is the Soviet Scud-B (~20 launchers, organized into a single brigade). The Scud-B essentially allows Syria

Table 15

Syrian Ballistic Missiles

Missile	Mobility	Guidance System	Accuracy (CEP in m)	Range (km)	Type and Weight of Warhead (kg)	Number of Launchers
FROG-7	Mobile	Unguided	500	70	HE, chemical [?] (435)	18
Scud-B	Mobile	Inertial	900–1,000	300	HE, chemical [?] (985)	20
SS-21	Mobile	Inertial plus terminal active radar homing	30 or 300	70	HE, chemical [?] (482)	18

[50]S. J. Lundin, "Chemical and Biological Warfare: Developments in 1988," *SIPRI Yearbook 1989*, p. 110; Cordesman, *Weapons of Mass Destruction*, pp. 146–148.

to target almost all of Israel, northern and western Iraq, the southern and eastern portions of Turkey, and Cyprus. Syria also has shorter-range FROG-7s and SS-21s; the latter missile is important because its active radar homing capabilities in the terminal phase give it high accuracy. It has been described as possessing a CEP of either 30 or 300 meters. Either figure makes it much more accurate than the Scud; if it does indeed have a CEP of 30 meters, it becomes a sophisticated counterforce weapon. And if armed with chemical warheads, it allows Syria to interdict front-line Israeli military installations, thereby freeing the Syrian air force for other missions.

Because ballistic missiles are particularly important to Syrian strategy, Syria has embarked on a wide-ranging effort to secure longer-range weapons. In 1986–1987, it sought to acquire the Soviet SS-23, a weapon with a 500-km range, but was not successful. Since then, it attempted to develop contacts with Libya, North Korea, and China for additional weapons.[51] The Libyan connection has atrophied, but in 1990 it was reported that Syria did indeed acquire some 35–50 extended-range Scud-Bs and 20 mobile launchers from North Korea as part of a total order of some 150 missiles.[52] These extended-range Scud-Bs, sometimes identified as Scud-Cs, have a range of 500 km and are armed with a 700-kg warhead. The accuracy of the missile is said to be better than that associated with the standard Scud. A missile of this range would enable Syria to target northern and western Iraq, including Baghdad; all of Israel and most of the Sinai; and all of southeastern Turkey, just short of Ankara. The Syrian–North Korean collaboration, which reportedly now also includes Iran, will only grow in importance in the coming decade.[53] In March 1992, several additional shipments of North Korean Scuds bound for Iran—but whose ultimate destination was Syria—were detected.[54]

Syria is also known to be interested in the even longer-range indigenous North Korean missile called Labour-1 or Nodong-1. The

---

[51]A good survey of Syrian missile procurement efforts can be found in Joseph S. Bermudez, Jr., "Syria's Acquisition of North Korean 'Scuds,'" *Jane's Intelligence Review*, June 1991, pp. 249–251.

[52]"Unclassified Projects: Offensive Weapons," *Jane's Strategic Weapons Systems*, Issue 12.

[53]"Syria and Iran Pool SRBM Resources," *Flight International*, October 22, 1991, p. 15.

[54]"Syria: Army," Periscope database, April 28, 1992.

Nodong is described as having a 1,000-km range and armed with a 1,000-kg warhead. A missile of this range, if based near Aleppo in northwestern Syria, would reach just beyond the Turkish Straits; if based in southeastern Syria, it would reach important Saudi targets as far south as King Khalid Military City.

Syria is also rumored to have reached agreement with China for the 600-km-range M-9 missile, but the exact status of this agreement is not clear.

Cruise missiles. Syrian cruise missiles—Styx—are deployed mainly aboard its naval vessels, though Syria also has shore batteries that consist of both Styx and Sepal missiles. The Syrian navy possesses a very small order of battle: its principal combatants are brown-water missile craft. Syrian missile-carrying forces consist of eighteen missile-armed patrol boats: the four Osa Is are each armed with four SS-N-2A Styx missiles, while the remainder, the ten Osa IIs, are each armed with four SS-N-2C Styx. There are also four *Komar*-class missile boats, each armed with two SS-N-2A Styx missiles.

The cruise missiles in the Syrian inventory are used mainly for anti-shipping missions, but the long range of the SSC-1B Sepal (460 km) lends itself to the anti-land-attack mission as well. For missions at maximum range, however, the inertial navigation system needs updates from aircraft or helicopter. There is also a reconnaissance drone, DR-3, based on the body of the SSC-1 Sepal: some units are possessed by Syria, and at least one is known to have been shot down by the Israelis.

The SS-N-2 Styx, which exists in shipboard and coastal battery versions, has a shorter range than the Sepal. It could be modified for land-attack purposes, but Syria is not considered to have the technical capability to undertake such modifications.

One source indicates that Syria is working on an indigenously produced cruise missile,[55] but no corroboration of this claim is found elsewhere in the literature. Syria was very impressed with the way

---

[55]Eisenstadt, "Syria's Strategic Weapons," p. 172.

Table 16

Syrian Cruise Missiles

Missile	Type	Launch Platform	Number of Platforms	Missile Range (km)	Guidance and Missile Accuracy	Type of Warhead (weight in kg)
SS-N-2C Styx	SSM	Ship	10	83	Autopilot with active radar/IR homing	HE (513)
SS-N-2A Styx	SSM	Ship	8	46	Autopilot with active radar/IR homing	HE (513)
SSC-1B Sepal	SSM	Mobile coastal battery	1 battalion: 18 launchers	460	Inertial with active radar homing and midcourse update	HE (1,000)
SSC-3 Styx	SSM	Mobile coastal battery	1 battalion: 18 launchers	80–100+	Autopilot with active radar/IR homing	HE (513)

cruise missiles were used during the Gulf War, and there have been recent reports that Syria and Iran have initiated a joint cruise missile development program with Chinese and North Korean technology.[56] Such a program appears consistent with the growing collaboration between Syria and Iran.

Aircraft. All aircraft capable of strike and ground-attack missions are deployed with the Syrian air force, which is exclusively Soviet equipped. The most significant aircraft in the strike component is the Soviet SU-24 Fencer, with a fairly large component of MiG-23BNs completing the ground-attack contingent.

The most capable strike aircraft in the Syrian inventory consists of the SU-24 Fencer, which has a low-level penetration capability. When flying a higher profile, the Fencer can reach ranges exceeding

---

[56]"Flashpoints," *Jane's Defence Weekly*, December 11, 1993, p. 18.

Table 17

Syrian Combat Aircraft

Aircraft	Primary Mission	Approximate Combat Radius	Approximate Maximum Payload	Types of Weapons Carried	Number
SU-24 Fencer	Dedicated GA	174–565 nm[a]	8,000 kg	General-purpose bombs; rockets; AAMs; ASMs	20
MiG-23 BN	Dedicated GA	378–620 nm[b]	3,000 kg	General-purpose bombs; rockets; AAMs; ASMs	60 (includes trainers)
SU-20/22	Dedicated GA	240–370 nm[c]	4,250 kg	General-purpose bombs; rockets; AAMs; ASMs	90
MiG-21 MF/bis	Interceptor with visual GA capability	200–400 nm[d]	~1,500 kg	AAMs: AA-2; AA-6; 250- and 500-kg bombs and assorted rockets	150 + 50 trainers
MiG-23 MF	Interceptor with visual GA capability	378–620 nm[b]	3,000 kg	AAMs	80
MiG-25	Dedicated interceptor	675–933 nm	3,000 kg	AAMs only	30 + 5 trainers
MiG-29	Interceptor with visual GA capability	~250 nm	3,000 kg	AAMs, bombs, rockets and submunition dispensers	20

[a]The 174-nm radius refers to a low-low-low profile. The 565-nm radius refers to a high-low-high profile with 3,000 kg of weapons and two external fuel tanks.

[b]The 378-nm radius presumes the aircraft carries 2,000 kg of bombs. The 620-nm radius is based on an ordnance load of six AAMs.

[c]The 240-nm radius presumes the aircraft to be carrying a 2,000-kg bomb load with external fuel and flying a low-low-low profile. The 370-nm radius presumes the same loads but a high-low-high profile.

[d]The 200-nm radius presumes the aircraft to be carrying four 250-kg bombs. The 400-nm radius presumes the aircraft to be carrying two 250-kg bombs and external drop tanks.

600 nm; in such missions, its reach rivals all but the longest-range SSM known to be of interest to Syria. With the Fencer, Syria can deliver conventional and chemical warheads to over half of Egypt, the northern half of Saudi Arabia, all of Turkey, and even the eastern half of Greece. Syria is known to be negotiating for additional Fencers, and Israeli sources suggest that 40 MiG-29s and 24 Fencers were contracted after the Gulf War.[57]

The MiG-23BNs and SU-20/22s have much shorter combat radii, in the 300-nm and 200-nm class respectively; with appropriate basing, the MiG-23s could reach Cairo, Baghdad, and Ankara with useful weapon loads.

Artillery and battlefield rocket systems.   Syrian artillery systems comprise exclusively Soviet equipment.

Syria has large numbers of diverse artillery systems, the largest number of which (650) is the Russian M-1946 with a 27-km range. Syria also has a tiny number of longer-range (30 km) large-caliber (180 mm) artillery (10 tubes), but the bulk of the artillery force can reach effective ranges of 11–27 km. At such ranges, Syrian artillery has essentially little more than operational-level significance; it would be most useful in border operations against Israel, Iraq, and Turkey. Syria also has a significant number of MRL systems, but these systems too have only tactical or at best operational-level significance.

Syria is known to stockpile a large number of tube- and rocket-delivered chemical munitions, but as noted earlier, these weapons do not have any strategic reach.

---

[57]"Syria: Air Force," Periscope database, April 28, 1992.

Table 18

Syrian Artillery and Battlefield Rockets

Weapon System	Type	Caliber	Range	Munitions Capability	Maximum Rate of Fire	Number
Russian M-1931/37	Towed	122 mm	20.8 km	HE, APHE, smoke	5–6 rds/min	100 (in store)
Russian M-1938	Towed	122 mm	11.8 km	HE, HEAT, smoke, illuminating	5–6 rds/min	150
Russian D-30	Towed	122 mm	15.3 km	HE, HEAT, smoke, illuminating	7–8 rds/min	500
Russian M-1946	Towed	130 mm	27 km	HE, APHE	6–7 rds/min	800
Russian D-20	Towed	152 mm	17.3 km	HE, APHE, chemical	4 rds/min	20
Russian M-1937	Towed	152 mm	17.3 km	HE, APHE	4 rds/min	50
Russian S-23	Towed	180 mm	30.4 km	HE, HE-frag, nuclear	1 rd/min	10
Russian 2S1	SP	122 mm	15.3 km	HE, HEAT, smoke, illuminating	5–8 rds/min	400
Russian 2S3	SP	152 mm	18.5 km	HE, HEAT, HE/RAP, incendiary, smoke, illuminating, nuclear	4 rds/min	50
Russian BM-21	MRL: 40 tubes	122 mm	14/20 km	HE, smoke, incendiary, chemical	Reload time: 10 min	280
Chinese Type 63	MRL: 12 tubes	107 mm	8.3 km	HE, HE-incendiary, HE-frag		200

IRAQ

WMD Potential or Capabilities

Nuclear facilities. Iraq's nuclear ambitions and the extent of its covert nuclear weapons acquisition program have been amply documented since the Gulf War.[58]

Iraq had three research reactors. The Osiraq, Tammuz I reactor, which used light water/highly enriched uranium and was rated at 40 MWt, is nonoperational, having been destroyed by Israel in June 1981 before startup. The future status of this facility is uncertain.

The Isis, Tammuz II is a pool-type reactor and also used light water/highly enriched uranium. It is supposed to have gone critical since 1987 and was rated at 500 kW steady power. The reactor and fuel (80 percent enriched U^{235}) were supplied by France. This reactor was shut down in March 1991.

The IRT-5000 was also a pool-type reactor using light water/highly enriched uranium, rated at 5 MWt. It was reported to have gone critical in 1967 and was fueled with 80 percent enriched U^{235}. Both the reactor and fuel were supplied by the Soviet Union. This reactor was shut down in March 1991.

Iraq is known to have a uranium mining site at Akashat and another exploratory mine near Najar. A small quantity of ore was mined from the latter facility before it flooded in late 1990. Iraq also had uranium extraction and purification facilities at Al Qaim, but these were destroyed during the Gulf War. Production facilities for uranium tetrachloride feedstocks also existed at Al Jasira, but these facilities too were damaged during the war. Iraq is also known to have acquired uranium oxide concentrate ("yellowcake") from Portugal, Brazil, Niger, and Italy,[59] and hundreds of tons of bulk nuclear materials were discovered by IAEA teams in the aftermath of the Gulf conflict.

---

[58]Tim Ripley, "Iraq's Nuclear Weapons Programme," *Jane's Intelligence Review,* December 1992, pp. 554–558; Holly Porteous, "Unravelling the Puzzle of Iraq's Nuclear Programme," *Jane's Defence Weekly,* October 5, 1991, pp. 602–603.

[59]Spector and Smith, *Nuclear Ambitions,* p. 202.

Most of these materials, imported clandestinely, were intended for use in Iraq's covert enrichment program.

The evidence uncovered in the aftermath of the Gulf War revealed that Iraq was pursuing multiple paths to acquiring fissile materials, consisting mainly of enriching natural uranium through industrial processes. The main approaches evidently focused on electromagnetic isotope separation and gas centrifuge enrichment, though other approaches, like chemical exchange isotope separation and gaseous diffusion, were apparently also initiated. Iraqi research on chemical exchange separation was apparently linked to lithium-6 enrichment, suggesting an interest in thermonuclear or at least hybrid nuclear weapons.[60] The Iraqi nuclear program currently faces an enforced pause, but Iraqi behavior with respect to complying with the relevant UN resolutions suggests that the nuclear weapons program will be reinitiated the moment external constraints dissipate.

Biological facilities. Iraq is identified by several sources as having an undeclared offensive biological-weapons program.[61] Early reports that Iraq might have used mycotoxins against the Kurds are probably false, but most agree that anthrax and botulin toxins are among the primary agents of interest to the Iraqis. Iraq also appears to be conducting research into typhoid, cholera, tularemia, and equine encephalitis.[62] In October 1990, the CIA announced that Iraq was producing biological weapons. Iraq is known to have a major biological-weapons research facility at Salman Pak and perhaps additional facilities at Samarra and at one other location west of Baghdad.[63]

European suppliers dominate the list of international suppliers of biological-weapons equipment to Iraq.

---

[60]A concise survey of the Iraqi nuclear infrastructure aimed at weapons development can be found in Leonard S. Spector et al., *Tracking Nuclear Proliferation*, Washington, D.C.: Carnegie Endowment for International Peace, 1995, pp. 128–133.

[61]Carus, "The Poor Man's Atomic Bomb?"; Fairhall, "Eleven Countries"; U.S. Arms Control and Disarmament Agency, "Adherence to and Compliance with Arms Control Agreements"; and Harvey J. McGeorge, "Chemical Addiction," *Defense and Foreign Affairs*, April 1989.

[62]*Washington Times,* January 19, 1989, p. A-8.

[63]Cordesman, *Weapons of Mass Destruction*, p. 81.

Chemical facilities. Iraq has probably been the most extensive user of chemical weapons in the Middle East. Iraqi chemical weapons have been used against the Kurds and against the Iranians during the Iran-Iraq War.[64] Iraqi chemical-weapons research and production has focused mainly on producing a variety of mustard and nerve gases. Iraq developed a limited capability to produce mustard gas and fill artillery projectiles and mortar rounds by the late 1970s, but production capabilities do not seem to have appreciated sufficiently by the early 1980s. One source indicates that Iraqi mustard gas, delivered through 250-kg bombs purchased from Spain, revealed exceptionally pure gas. This suggests that Iraq was still relying on laboratory rather than large-scale industrial production.[65] The need to produce large quantities of mustard gas apparently led to new efforts to acquire European technology in the post-1982 period, and these efforts ultimately resulted in a mustard gas plant being constructed at Akashat, 370 km from Baghdad. By 1988, Iraq also developed the ability to produce some precursors for nerve gas.

Major Iraqi chemical-weapons production facilities existed at Salman Pak, which apparently experimented with cyanide, hydrogen-cyanide, cyanogen-chloride, and Lewisite, as well as nerve, mustard, and CS gases; and at Samarra, which was the largest single Iraqi production facility for mustard gas and which produced Tabun and Sarin nerve gases as well. Other facilities existed at Rutbah, which produced organophosphate feedstocks for nerve gas production at a complex called "Project 9320" and at Fallujah, which both produced Sarin and VX nerve gases and loaded them into artillery and rocket shells. Still other facilities have been identified at Al Iskandariyah, Baiji, and Karbala.

Iraq had developed a variety of delivery systems for its chemical weapons, including 250-kg air-delivered bombs; 90 mm air-to-surface rockets; 120 mm mortars; 122 mm, 130 mm, and 155 mm artillery; BM-21 MLRS; and warheads for its Scud missiles.

---

[64]Colleen Nash, "Chemwar in the Third World," *Air Force Magazine*, January 1990, pp. 80–83; Lee Waters, "Chemical Weapons in the Iran/Iraq War," *Military Review*, October 1990, pp. 57–63.

[65]Cordesman, *Weapons of Mass Destruction*, p. 66.

Foreign collaboration and presence. No open foreign collaboration with Iraq has existed since the aftermath of the Gulf War. Individual volunteers from Russia have been listed, however, and the presence of some Chinese personnel is reported but not confirmed.

Delivery Systems

Ballistic missiles. Iraq's ballistic missile arsenal consisted primarily of the Scud-B (in several indigenously modified variants) and FROG-7 rockets. These weapons are due to be destroyed under the terms of the UN resolutions ending the Gulf War, but the basic data are recorded below to provide some baselines about the reach of Iraq's WMD delivery capabilities.

Table 19

Iraqi Ballistic Missiles

Missile	Mobility	Guidance System	Accuracy (CEP in m)	Range (km)	Type of Warhead (weight in kg)	Number of Launchers
FROG-7	Mobile	Unguided	500	70	HE, chemical [?] (435)	Unknown
Laith 90 (modified FROG-7)	Mobile	Unguided	?	90	Cluster munitions	Unknown
Scud-B	Mobile	Inertial	900–1,000	300	HE, chemical [?] (985)	Unknown
Al Hussein (modified Scud-B)	Mobile	Inertial	1,000	650	HE, chemical (500)	Unknown
Al Abbas (modified Scud-B: development, now terminated?)	Mobile	Inertial	1,500–3,000	900	HE, chemical [?] (350)	Unknown
Al Aabed (derived from Tammouz satellite launcher: development, now terminated?)	?	Inertial	?	2,000	HE [?], chemical [?] (750)	Unknown

The principal missile in the Iraqi arsenal was the Al Hussein, the modified Scud-B with a range of about 650 km, 96 of which were launched against various targets during the Gulf War. The Al Hussein essentially allowed Iraq to reach targets as far away as Tehran and Jerusalem. The Al Abbas, which was test fired, would have extended Iraq's reach to northeastern Egypt, northern Saudi Arabia (including Cairo and Riyadh), western Iran, and eastern Turkey (including Ankara). The Al Aabed would have let Iraq target Pakistan, Afghanistan, southwestern and European Russia (including Moscow), Greece, and southern Italy. All these programs are now terminated but would in all probability be rapidly resurrected as soon as the constraints imposed by the Gulf War cease-fire dissipate.

In addition to these indigenous programs, Iraq pursued several international ballistic missile programs. Iraq was involved in the Argentinean Condor program (now defunct) and showed some interest in the Brazilian Avibras SS-300 missile.

Cruise missiles. The Iraqi cruise missile inventory consists of an assortment of cruise missiles ranging from the Soviet Styx on board its single surviving *Osa*-class missile boat (four SS-N-2As), to French ASMs like the Exocet, to its own indigenously produced ASMs and SSMs like the Ababil and the Faw.

The Iraqi cruise missile inventory was sharply reduced thanks to the high losses suffered during the Gulf War. Iraq is known to have lost 14 combat, 4 amphibious, and 7 auxiliary vessels during the conflict.

The Iraqis are known to have had quite an active cruise missile development program, but the bulk of the effort essentially consisted of developing longer-range versions of the Soviet Styx for coastal launch. The Faw series essentially consists of lengthened Styx missiles designed to reach ranges of 80, 150, and 200 km. The guidance and propulsion systems remain identical to the Styx. Utilizing the missile at the extremity of its range requires target updates provided either by aircraft or helicopter. Some Faw 70s were fired at ship targets during the Gulf War, without success.

The Ababil ASM was a developmental program that most sources suggest was a modified Italian Mirach 100 target drone. The missile is not known to have been flight tested, and its future status is uncertain.

Table 20

Iraqi Cruise Missiles

Missile	Type	Launch Platform	Number of Platforms	Missile Range (km)	Guidance and Missile Accuracy	Type of Warhead (weight in kg)
SS-N-2A Styx	SSM	Ship	1	46	Autopilot with active radar/IR homing	HE (513)
AM-39	ASM	Aircraft helicopter	?	50	Inertial with active radar	HE shaped charge fragmentation (165)
C-601	ASM	Aircraft	?	80	Semi-active radar with terminal active radar homing	HE (510)
Faw 70	SSM	Coastal battery	?	80	Autopilot with active radar homing	HE, chemical (500)
Faw 150	SSM	Coastal battery	?	150	Autopilot with active radar homing	HE, chemical (500)
Faw 200	SSM	Coastal battery	?	200	Autopilot with active radar homing	HE, chemical (500)
Ababil (appears to be based on Mirach 100 target drone)	ASM	Aircraft	?	500	Inertial [?], command guidance with midcourse update [?] with terminal visual/IR homing [?]	Information not available

Aircraft. All aircraft capable of strike and ground-attack missions are deployed with the Iraqi air force, though the Iraqi army does have a substantial contingent of armed helicopters. The exact numbers of forces surviving the Gulf War is unclear, but the kinds of aircraft are listed in Table 21, again to provide some sort of baseline with respect to the reach of Iraqi capabilities.

The longest-range aircraft in the Iraqi inventory are the TU-16s and TU-22s, both of which were used in the Iran-Iraq War. These are antiquated aircraft that would be unable to penetrate any modern air defense system. The Mirage F1, followed by the MiG-23BN and the MiG-27, represent the aircraft of next-longest range: the Mirage is a 400-nm–class aircraft, whereas the Migs can carry useful loads in the range of 200–300 nm. Most of these aircraft are known to be in poor shape as a result of the international arms embargo against Iraq.

Iraq also lost considerable numbers of modern attack aircraft to Iran. These aircraft flew to Iran during the Gulf War, and some have now been inducted into the Iranian air force. Among the aircraft held by Iran are 24 SU-24 Fencers, 24 Mirage F-1s, 12 MiG-23 Floggers, 4 MiG-29 Fulcrums, and over 40 SU-20/22 Fitters.

The future of the Iraqi air force is an open question at this point.

Artillery and battlefield rocket systems. The Iraqi artillery arm consists of assorted Russian, South African, U.S., Austrian, and some indigenous tubes. The MRL systems consist of Russian equipment, Brazilian systems produced under license, and some indigenous systems.

The maximum range of Iraqi tube artillery is 27 km, and there are numerous artillery systems, both towed and self-propelled, with ranges of 11–27 km. Iraqi artillery can thus reach operational-level ranges and is known to be one of the principal systems for delivering chemical weapons. Various 130 mm, 155 mm, and BM-21 MRL systems have been used for chemical delivery. The modification of a BM-21 rocket to carry chemical agents was apparently indigenous.

Iraq also had a large number of MRL systems under development. The Ababeel 50 and Ababeel 100 were fairly long-range systems with maximum ranges of 50 and 100 km respectively. Both systems, however, were designed to carry antipersonnel and antitank submunitions, but there is no reason why these systems could not be equipped with a chemical warhead. The Sajeel series had a maximum range of 60 km, and these too were armed with conventional submunitions.

Table 21

Iraqi Combat Aircraft

Aircraft	Primary Mission	Approximate Combat Radius	Approximate Maximum Payload	Types of Weapons Carried	Number
H-6/TU-16	Bomber	3,108 nm	9,000 kg	General-purpose bombs; ASMs	6
TU-22	Bomber	700–1,185 nm	12,000 kg	General-purpose bombs; ASMs	Included in above total
J-6	Light attack	370 nm[a]	~1,000 kg	Mixed fuel, bomb and rocket loads	130
MiG-23 BN	Dedicated GA	378–620 nm[b]	3,000 kg	General-purpose bombs; rockets; AAMs; ASMs	Included in above total
MiG-27	Dedicated GA	378–620 nm[b]	4,000 kg	General-purpose bombs; rockets; AAMs; ASMs	Included in above total
Mirage F-1EQ5	Multirole fighter with GA capability	230–750 nm[c]	6,500 kg	General-purpose bombs; rockets; AAMs; ASMs	Included in above total
SU-7 SU-20/22	Dedicated GA	240–370 nm[d]	4,250 kg	General-purpose bombs; rockets; AAMs; ASMs	Included in above total
SU-25	CAS aircraft		4,400 kg	General-purpose bombs; rockets; AAMs; ASMs	Included in above total

Table 21—continued

Aircraft	Primary Mission	Approximate Combat Radius	Approximate Maximum Payload	Types of Weapons Carried	Number
J-7	Multirole fighter with visual GA capability	200–324 nm	~1,500 kg	General-purpose bombs; rockets; AAMs	180
MiG-21 MF/bis	Interceptor with visual GA capability	200–400 nm[e]	~1,500 kg	AAMs: AA-2; AA-6; 250- and 500-kg bombs and assorted rockets	Included in above total
MiG-25	Dedicated interceptor	675–933 nm		AAMs only	Included in above total
MiG-29	Interceptor with visual GA capability	~250 nm	3,000 kg	AAMs, bombs, rockets, and submunition dispensers	Included in above total

[a] Assumes 800-liter external tanks and air-to-air weapons only.

[b] The 378-nm radius presumes the aircraft carries 2,000 kg of bombs. The 620-nm radius is based on an ordnance load of six AAMs.

[c] The 230-nm radius presumes a high-low-high profile with a 3,500-kg bomb load. The 750-nm radius presumes a high-low-high profile with a 500-kg bomb load and three external tanks. If a low-low-low profile is considered with a bomb load of about 1,500 kg and two external tanks, the combat radius of the Mirage F-1 is roughly 325 nm.

[d] The 240-nm radius presumes the aircraft to be carrying a 2,000-kg bomb load with external fuel and flying a low-low-low profile. The 370-nm radius presumes the same loads but a high-low-high profile.

[e] The 200-nm radius presumes the aircraft to be carrying four 250-kg bombs. The 400-nm radius presumes two 250-kg bombs and external drop tanks.

Table 22

Iraqi Artillery and Battlefield Rockets

Weapon System	Type	Caliber	Range	Munitions Capability	Maximum Rate of Fire	Number
M-56 Pack	Towed	105 mm	10.5 km	HE, HEAT, smoke, illuminating, chemical	8 rds/min	1,500
Russian D-74	Towed	122 mm	23.9 km	HE, APHE	6–7 rds/min	Included in above total
Russian D-30/ Saddam	Towed	122 mm	15.3 km	HE, HEAT, smoke, illuminating	7–8 rds/min	Included in above total
Russian M-1938	Towed	122 mm	11.8 km	HE, HEAT, smoke, illuminating	5–6 rds/min	Included in above total
Russian M-1946/ Type 59-1	Towed	130 mm	27 km	HE, APHE	6–7 rds/min	Included in above total
South African G-5	Towed	155 mm	30 km	HE, smoke, illuminating	3 rds/min	Included in above total
Austrian GHN-45	Towed	155 mm	30.3 km	HE, HEAT, smoke, illuminating	7 rds/min	Included in above total
U.S. M-114	Towed	155 mm	14.6 km	HE, smoke, illuminating, chemical	2 rds/min	Included in above total
Russian 2S1	SP	122 mm	15.3 km	HE, HEAT, smoke, illuminating	5–8 rds/min	230

Table 22—continued

Weapon System	Type	Caliber	Range	Munitions Capability	Maximum Rate of Fire	Number
Russian 2S3	SP	152 mm	18.5 km	HE, HEAT, HE/RAP, incendiary, smoke, illuminating, nuclear	4 rds/min	Included in above total
M-109A1/A2	SP	155 mm	18.1 km	HE, ICM, smoke, illuminating, nuclear, chemical	3–4 rds/ min	N/A
Portable rocket launcher system	MRL: 12 tubes	107 mm	8 km	HE		250
Russian BM-21	MRL: 40 tubes	122 mm	14/20 km	HE, smoke, incendiary, chemical	Reload time: 10 min	Included in above total
Sajeel 30 (locally produced Brazilian ASTROS II/SS-30)	MRL	127 mm	30 km	HE		Included in above total
Sajeel 40 (locally produced Brazilian ASTROS II/SS-40)	MRL	180 mm	35 km	ICM		Included in above total
Sajeel 60 (locally produced Brazilian ASTROS II/SS-60)	MRL	300 mm	60 km	ICM		Included in above total
Ababeel 50	MRL	262 mm	50 km	Submunition dispensing: mines; cluster		Included in above total
Ababeel 100	MRL	400 mm	100 km	Submunition dispensing: antitank; cluster		
BM-13/16	MRL	132 mm				

IRAN

WMD Potential or Capabilities

Nuclear facilities. Prior to 1979, Iran had the most advanced nuclear program in the Middle East. This program, initiated by the Shah, was aimed at developing a nuclear infrastructure that would both generate nuclear power and provide the wherewithal to produce nuclear weapons. This ambitious program had atrophied after the Iranian revolution, but a steady effort has been made during the past decade to resurrect it, including the research effort aimed at producing nuclear weapons.

Iran has four nuclear research facilities and one training reactor. Among the former is a safeguarded 5-MWt pool reactor located at the Nuclear Research Center in Tehran. The reactor and fuel (highly enriched uranium) were originally supplied by the United States; in May 1987, however, Argentina agreed to modify the reactor to utilize low-enriched uranium, which it has since supplied under safeguards. The other facilities at Isfahan include two subcritical assemblies and one tank in pool reactor, the fuel for which is supplied by China. An additional research reactor is under construction.

Iran also has three nonoperational power reactors. The Bushehr I and Bushehr II are light-water/low-enriched-uranium reactors designed to produce 1,300 MWe of power. They were supplied by the German firm Kraftwerk Union; construction on both reactors was suspended and both facilities were damaged by Iraqi air strikes in 1987 and 1988. No fuel was supplied to either reactor. The third facility, the Darkouin light-water/low-enriched-uranium reactor designed to produce 935 MWe, was supplied by France under safeguards. Construction halted in 1979 and no fuel was supplied.

Iran has been negotiating with both Russia and China for the supply of additional power reactors, and two agreements for purchase were signed in September 1992. Russia has agreed to sell Iran two 440-MW water-cooled, water-moderated reactors, and China has agreed to assist Iran in constructing two 300-MW reactors at Darkouin.[66] The implementation of both agreements, however, is beset by uncertainty.

Iran is known to have about 5,000 tons of reasonably assured yellow cake reserves in Yazd province. Iran announced plans to set up a uranium ore processing plant in Yazd and this facility was under construction as of 1989.

In October 1988, the speaker of the Iranian parliament, Akbar Rafsanjani, called for the development of nuclear weapons, a development no doubt partially conditioned by the war with Iraq. In early 1989, the Director of Naval Intelligence informed Congress that Iran was "actively pursuing" a nuclear weapons capability. Iran is known to have a nuclear cooperation agreement with Pakistan, and there has been speculation about Iranian efforts to seek assistance from India, North Korea, and China.[67]

In 1992, it was reported that Iran had acquired four nuclear weapons from Kazakhstan, of which two were operational. These were reputedly 40-kt warheads designed for the Scud-C missile, some of which Iran is known to possess. The others weapons included a 50-kt aerial bomb designed for carriage by a MiG-27 and a 0.1-kt artillery shell.[68] The authenticity of this report is suspect; both the Kazakh government and the U.S. State Department denied the sale had taken place, but rumors about Iranian nuclear purchases have been widespread. U.S. government analysts today believe that Iran could produce nuclear weapons within a 5–10 year period.[69]

---

[66]Betsy Perabo, "A Chronology of Iran's Nuclear Program," *Eye on Supply*, Fall 1992, p. 64; "Agreements on Nuclear Cooperation Ratified," *FBIS-NES*, April 14, 1993, pp. 48–49.

[67]Cordesman, *Weapons of Mass Destruction*, p. 105. See also David Segal, "Iran Speeds Up Nuclear Bomb Development," *Journal of Defense and Diplomacy*, 1989, pp. 52–55.

[68]James Wyllie, "Iran's Quest for Security and Influence," *Jane's Intelligence Review*, July 1993, pp. 311–312.

[69]Chris Hedges, "Iran May Be Able to Build an Atomic Bomb in 5 years, U.S. and Israeli Officials Fear," *The New York Times*, January 5, 1995, p. 10.

Biological facilities. Iran is sometimes identified as a state pursuing offensive biological-weapons programs, but no universal consensus exists on this matter.[70] The October 1988 statement of Rafsanjani included an explicit call to produce biological weapons. Whether this statement had any practical consequences is unknown. At least one source suggests that Iran has an "extensive laboratory and research capability,"[71] but this may simply describe a pharmaceutical infrastructure that could be put to dual use. Iran probably has a low-level program of biological-weapons research, but no major dedicated facilities have been identified in the unclassified literature.

Chemical facilities. Iran embarked on a chemical-weapons program as a result of the Iran-Iraq War and is not known to have employed chemical weapons prior to 1984. The early use of chemical weapons most probably involved captured Iraqi rounds, but a crash effort to domestically produce chemical weapons was initiated at about that time. By 1986–1987, Iran began to produce sufficient quantities of chemical agents to load its own weapons, and production facilities have been identified at Damghan, Mahshar, and Qazvin. The CIA suggests that Iranian capabilities at this time included the capability to manufacture vesicants like mustard gas and blood gases like hydrogen cyanide, phosgene, and chlorine gas. These agents were delivered through air-delivered bombs and artillery shells and were used sporadically against Iraq in 1987–1988.

Iran is suspected of having at least two research and production facilities capable of manufacturing both mustard and nerve gases, including V-agents. According to one source, Iran is capable of manufacturing up to five tons of chemical-weapons agents per month.[72] Such agents, at present, can be delivered through bombs and artillery, and Iran is known to be investigating the possibility of delivering chemical agents through SSMs. A recent news report cites West German intelligence sources as reporting that a secret complex de-

---

[70]The relevant works by Seth Carus, Elisa Harris, and the Russian Federation Foreign Intelligence Service report cited earlier identify Iran as pursuing a biological-weapons program.

[71]Cordesman, *Weapons of Mass Destruction,* p. 29.

[72]"Missiles Armed With Chemical Weapons in Sight," *The Observer,* March 13, 1988, p. 23.

signed for the production of nerve gases, primarily Sarin and Tabun, is on the verge of completion with assistance from Indian chemical companies.[73]

Foreign collaboration and presence. The most significant foreign collaboration with Iran currently consists of Chinese and North Korean assistance in the Iranian ballistic missile program. The number of personnel stationed in Iran is not known, but Chinese nuclear technicians are known to be among them. Iran is known to have advisers and perhaps nuclear scientists/technicians from Pakistan, pilots from Russia, and some nuclear scientists/technicians from India.

Delivery Systems

Ballistic missiles. The Iranian ballistic missile inventory consists principally of the Soviet Scud in two variants and an assortment of indigenously produced unguided rockets.

Iran acquired its earliest order of Scud-Bs from Syria and Libya in 1985–1986. In 1987–1988, Iran acquired additional Scud-Bs from North Korea, and these weapons were used extensively in the "War of the Cities." Iran is also known to have Scud-Cs, which are longer-range variants of the Scud-B. One source estimates that about 100 of these systems are currently in service.[74] Using either type of weapon, Iran can target nearly two-thirds of Iraq, eastern Turkey, and western Afghanistan and Pakistan. In January 1991, the Iranian government announced that it had a ballistic missile production capability, and this is taken by authoritative sources to mean that Iran can locally manufacture either or both the Scud-B and Scud-C.[75]

Iran's present capabilities are rather modest, but it has undertaken a variety of ballistic missile R&D programs designed to increase its

---

[73]Jamie Dettmer, "Tehran Building Deadly Gas Plant," *The Washington Times*, January 30, 1995, p. 1.

[74]Chalmers Hardenbergh (ed.), *The Arms Control Reporter 1993*, Brookline, MA: Institute for Defense and Disarmament Studies, 706.E.9.

[75]Tony Banks and James Bruce, "Iran Builds Its Strength," *Jane's Defence Weekly*, February 1, 1992, pp. 158–159.

Table 23

Iranian Ballistic Missiles

Missile	Mobility	Guidance System	Accuracy (CEP in m)	Range (km)	Type of Warhead (weight in kg)	Number of Launchers
CSS-8						20
Scud-B	Mobile	Inertial	900–1,000	300	HE, chemi-cal [?] (985)	6+ missiles
Scud-C (N. Kore-an manu-facture)	Mobile	Inertial	700	550	HE	
Iran-130	Mobile	Inertial [?]	Unknown	130	HE [?]	Under develop-ment [?]
Nazeat (355 mm)	Mobile	Unguided	Unknown	90 km	HE (150)	
Shahin 2 (333 mm)	Mobile	Unguided	Unknown	20 km	HE (180)	
Oghab (230 mm)	Mobile	Unguided	Unknown	80 km	HE (70)	

strategic reach. Iran is known to be pursuing a variety of programs, including the "Tondar-68," with either China or North Korea or both. This program is designed to produce a missile of 1,000-km range capable of carrying a warhead of 400 to 1,000 kg. This program could be the same as the North Korean Labour-1 (Nodong-1), but it could also be derived from the Chinese M-18 design, which in turn was based on the Brazilian SS-1000. In either case, the fact remains that Iran has assiduously pursued relationships with both North Korea and China in search of missile systems capable of reaching anywhere from 300 to 1,300 km.[76] It must be expected that the longer-range weapons will be in Iranian service by the end of the century. Such a missile would allow Iran to target the eastern half of Turkey (almost reaching Ankara) and almost all of Saudi Arabia, including Riyadh.

---

[76]"Missile Deal Outlined," *FBIS-NES*, December 11, 1992, p. 48.

Besides these long-range ballistic missile research programs, Iran has also developed a series of shorter-range unguided artillery rockets and at least the first of three shorter-range guided missiles. The Nazeat, Shahin, and Oghab unguided artillery rockets with ranges from 20–90 km are currently armed with unitary HE warheads. These weapons allow Iranian artillery to influence the battlefield at the operational level, and there is no reason why they cannot be equipped with either chemical or biological warheads if Iran should so choose. The Iran-130/Mushak-120 is the first of a series of three solid-propelled, guided ballistic missiles. Between five and ten weapons were known to be fired in the "War of the Cities." The Iran-130 has a range of 130 km, and the sister weapons in the series, the Mushak-160 and -200, will have ranges of 160 km and 200 km respectively. These weapons are probably inertially guided but their accuracy is unknown.

Cruise missiles. The Iranian cruise missile inventory consists mainly of tactical antishipping cruise missiles deployed around surface vessels and in coastal batteries. The missile-carrying naval order of battle essentially comprises three UK *Vosper*-class frigates, each armed with five Sea Killer missiles and ten French Combattante II missile boats, some equipped to carry four Harpoon SSMs. There are also three known Silkworm missile sites, and Iran is known to possess some unknown number of Chinese C-801 missiles, which can be used both in the surface- and air-launched regime. Which launch platform is used for these missiles is not known.

The data suggest that Iran's interest in cruise missile systems is oriented primarily toward the coastal defense/sea denial role. All these weapons are designed primarily to attack ship targets, but missiles like the Harpoon and Silkworm could be modified to attack land targets. Modifying the latter weapon might be within the range of Iranian capabilities, but modifying the former would require outside assistance.

Iran is known to be pursuing an indigenous cruise missile development program in collaboration with Syria.

Table 24

Iranian Cruise Missiles

Missile	Type	Launch Platform	Number of Platforms	Missile Range (km)	Guidance and Missile Accuracy	Type of Warhead (weight in kg)
RGM-84 Harpoon	SSM	Ship	?	130	Inertial with active radar	HE (227)
Italian Seakiller	SSM	Ship	3	25	Beam rider: radio/optical command	HE (70)
CSS-C-2 Silkworm	SSM	Coastal battery	~3 sites each with 3–6 missiles	95	Autopilot with active radar homing	HE (513)
C-801	SSM/ ASM	Coastal battery [?]; aircraft [?]	?	50	Inertial with terminal active radar homing	HE semiarmor piercing (165)

Aircraft. All strike aircraft are deployed by the Iranian air force. The most capable aircraft in the inventory currently are the Soviet SU-24 Fencer and the U.S. F-4D/E Phantom. Aircraft with secondary strike capabilities include the U.S. F-5E and the Chinese F-7, but these are essentially short-legged aircraft with limited reach.

The Iranian air force, which was one of the most sophisticated regional forces during the reign of the Shah and which fell rapidly into disrepair thereafter, is currently involved in an intriguing, but systematic, modernization program. With the 30 SU-24s in the inventory, Iran has acquired an extremely able dedicated strike aircraft capable of low-level penetration. The SU-24 can carry a heavy weapons load beyond a 600-nm radius; at such ranges, Iran could target most of Turkey (including Ankara), most of the Saudi Arabian peninsula, and all of Iraq in the west, while reaching as far as western India in the east. Iran will extend its strike reach even further if the reported contract to purchase 12 TU-22M Backfire bombers is true. The Backfire can carry an enormous weapons load of up to 24,000 kg and has a combat radius of between 810 and 1,187 nm. Depending

Table 25
Iranian Combat Aircraft

Aircraft	Primary Mission	Approximate Combat Radius	Approximate Maximum Payload	Types of Weapons Carried	Number
F-4D/E	Multirole fighter with automated GA capability	429–618 nm[a]	7,250 kg	General-purpose bombs; rockets; AAMs; ASMs	60
SU-24 Fencer	Dedicated GA	174–565 nm[b]	8,000 kg	General-purpose bombs; rockets; AAMs; ASMs	30
F-5E/F	FGA	120–570 nm[c]	3,175 kg	General-purpose bombs; rockets; AAMs; ASMs: AGM-65B Maverick	60 + 20 trainers
F-14A	Interceptor with visual GA capability	~400 nm	6,577 kg	AAMs; general-purpose bombs	60
F-7 (Chinese MiG-21 version)	Interceptor with visual GA capability	100–200 nm	~1,500 kg	AAMs; general-purpose bombs; rockets	25 + 5 trainers
MiG-29	Interceptor with visual GA capability	~250 nm	3,000 kg	AAMs, bombs, rockets and submunition dispensers	30 + 5 trainers

[a]The 429-nm radius refers to aircraft flying defensive counterair missions. The 618-nm radius refers to aircraft flying interdiction missions.

[b]The 174-nm radius refers to a low-low-low profile. The 565-nm radius refers to a high-low-high profile with 3,000 kg of weapons and two external fuel tanks.

[c]The approximate combat radius depends, inter alia, on the type and weight of ordnance carried, the cruising profile, and the kind and number of external fuel tanks. The 120-nm combat radius presumes full ordnance load, two Sidewinder missiles, maximum internal fuel, five minutes of combat, and a low-low-low profile usually associated with covert ground-attack missions. The 570-nm figure, in contrast, presumes a fighter intercept mission with the aircraft carrying maximum internal fuel, two Sidewinder missiles, reserves for twenty minutes, and five minutes of combat with maximum engine power.

on the flight profile and the weight carried, this aircraft enables Iran to strike targets as far west as Greece and as far east as Bombay.

Iranian purchases of modern aircraft, especially from Russia and the other former Soviet republics, will only increase in the near future. Recent reports indicate that an $11 billion deal with Russia will provide additional MiG-29s, MiG-31s, and MiG-27s, as well as maritime reconnaissance and AWACS aircraft.

Artillery and battlefield rocket systems. Iranian tube and rocket artillery consists of a diverse collection of Russian Chinese, Austrian, South African, and some U.S. pieces.

All Iranian artillery essentially consists of weapons capable of delivering fire in the range of 11–30 km. A large number of Chinese pieces are identifiable in the inventory, illustrating the close links forged with China during the Iran-Iraq War. Artillery systems were a crucial means of delivering chemical weapons during the war and will remain so.

Table 26

Iranian Artillery and Battlefield Rockets

Weapon System	Type	Caliber	Range	Munitions Capability	Maximum Rate of Fire	Number
U.S. M-101	Towed	105 mm	11.2 km	HE, HEAT, smoke, chemical	8 rds/min	130
Ex-Yug M-56	Towed	105 mm	13 km	HE, HEAT, smoke, illuminating	6–7 rds/min	50
Russian D-30	Towed	122 mm	15.3 km	HE, HEAT, smoke, illuminating	7–8 rds/min	400
Chinese Type 54 (Russian M-1938)	Towed	122 mm	11.8 km	HE, HEAT, smoke, illuminating	5–6 rds/min	150
Russian M-1946/ Type 59-1	Towed	130 mm	27 km	HE, APHE	6–7 rds/min	800
Russian D-20 (M-1955)	Towed	152 mm	17.3 km	HE, APHE, chemical	4 rds/min	30
U.S. M-114	Towed	155 mm	14.6 km	HE, smoke, illuminating, chemical	2 rds/min	50
Austrian GHN-45	Towed	155 mm	30.3 km	HE, HEAT, smoke, illuminating	7 rds/min	~130
Chinese WA-021	Towed	155 mm	30 km	HE, smoke, illuminating	3–4 rds/min	50
U.S. M-115	Towed	203 mm	16.8 km	HE, chemical, nuclear	1 rd/2 min	~30

Table 26—continued

Weapon System	Type	Caliber	Range	Munitions Capability	Maximum Rate of Fire	Number
Russian 2S1	SP	122 mm	15.3 km	HE, HEAT, smoke, illuminating	5–8 rds/min	20
M-109	SP	155 mm	18.1 km	HE, smoke, illuminating, chemical	3–4 rds/min	~95
M-1978	SP	175 mm				15
M-107	SP	175 mm	32.7 km	HE, chemical	1 rd/min	20
M-110	SP	203 mm	16.8 km	HE, chemical, nuclear	1 rd/2 min	10
Chinese Type 63	MRL: 12 tubes	107 mm	8–10 km	HE, HE-incendiary, HE-frag	Reload time: 3 min	40
Russian BM-11		122 mm				5
Hadid Arash Noor	MRL					40
Russian BM-21	MRL: 40 tubes	122 mm	14/20 km	HE, smoke, incendiary, chemical	Reload time: 10 min	65
Russian BM-24	MRL: 12 tubes	240 mm	10.3 km	HE-frag, smoke, chemical		?

SELECTED BIBLIOGRAPHY

Aliboni, Roberto (ed.), *Southern European Security in the 1990s,* London: Pinter, 1992.

"Alliance Policy Framework on Proliferation of Weapons of Mass Destruction," Ministerial Meeting of the North Atlantic Council, Istanbul, June 9, 1994. Published in *NATO Review,* June 1994, pp. 28–29.

Arquilla, John, and Paul K. Davis, *Modeling Decisionmaking of Potential Proliferators as Part of Developing Counterproliferation Strategies,* Santa Monica, CA: RAND, MR-467, 1994.

Banks, Tony, and James Bruce, "Iran Builds Its Strength," *Jane's Defence Weekly,* February 1, 1992.

Beaver, Paul, "Nodong-1 Details Fuel New Fears in Asia," *Jane's Defence Weekly,* January 15, 1994.

Bermudez, Joseph S., Jr., "Ballistic Missile Development in Egypt," *Jane's Intelligence Review,* October 1992.

———, "Syria's Acquisition of North Korean 'Scuds,'" *Jane's Intelligence Review,* June 1991.

———, "Ballistic Ambitions Ascendant," *Jane's Defence Weekly,* April 10, 1993.

Blackwill, Robert D., and Albert Carnesale (eds.), *New Nuclear Nations: Consequences for U.S. Policy,* New York: Council on Foreign Relations, 1993.

Blunden, Margaret, "France After the Cold War: Inching Closer to the Alliance," *Defence Analysis*, Vol. 9, No. 3, pp. 259–270.

Brassey's Artillery of the World, New York: Bonanza Books, 1977.

Carus, W. Seth, "'The Poor Man's Atomic Bomb?' Biological Weapons in the Middle East." *Policy Papers*, No. 23, Washington, D.C.: The Washington Institute for Near East Policy, 1991.

———, *Ballistic Missiles in Modern Conflict*, New York: Praeger, 1991.

———, *Cruise Missile Proliferation in the 1990s*, Westport, CT: Praeger, 1992.

"Chinese Nuclear Weapons Reactor for Algeria." *Defence*, May 1991.

Cordesman, Anthony H., *Weapons of Mass Destruction in the Middle East*, London: Brassey's, 1991.

Douglass, Joseph, Jr., "Soviets Surge in Biochemical Warfare; West Remains Drugged with Apathy," *Armed Forces Journal International*, August 1988.

Eisenstadt, Michael, "Syria's Strategic Weapons," *Jane's Intelligence Review*, April 1993.

Fairhall, David, "Eleven Countries Defying Ban on Germ Weapons," *The Guardian*, September 5, 1991.

Fetter, Steve, "Ballistic Missiles and Weapons of Mass Destruction," *International Security*, Summer 1991.

"Flashpoints," *Jane's Defence Weekly*, December 11, 1993.

Focus on Libya, Washington, D.C.: PEMCON, Ltd., 1990.

"France Studies Non-Nuclear Deterrence," *International Defense Review*, February 1993, pp. 92–93.

Gander, Terry J., "Chemical Warfare Today," *Jane's Intelligence Review*, June 1992.

Garrity, Patrick J., *Why the Gulf War Still Matters: Foreign Perspectives on the War and the Future of International Security,* Los Alamos: Center for National Security Studies, 1993.

Gupta, Vipin, "Algeria Nuclear Ambitions," *International Defense Review,* April 1992.

Harris, Elisa, "Towards a Comprehensive Strategy for Halting Chemical and Biological Weapons Proliferation," *Arms Control: Contemporary Security Policy,* Vol. 12, No. 2, September 1991.

Harvey, John R., "Regional Ballistic Missiles and Advanced Strike Aircraft," *International Security,* Vol. 17, No. 2, Fall 1992.

Huntington, Samuel, "The Clash of Civilizations?" *Foreign Affairs,* Summer 1993.

"Iraq: Defense Organization/Strength," U.S. Naval Institute, Periscope database, July 15, 1993.

Jacobs, Gordon, and Tim McCarthy, "China's Missile Sales—Few Changes for the Future," *Jane's Intelligence Review,* December 1992.

Jane's Air-launched Weapons, various editions.

Jane's All the World's Aircraft, various editions.

Jane's Armor and Artillery, various editions.

Jane's Fighting Ships, various editions.

Jane's Strategic Weapons Systems, various editions.

"Jottings," *Asian Defense Journal,* March 1992.

Kessler, Richard, "Panel to Guide Nuclear Technology Sales from Argentina to Algeria," *Nucleonics Week,* May 7, 1987.

Knoth, Artur, "GPS Technology and Third World Missiles," *International Defense Review,* May 1992.

Lellouche, Pierre, "France in Search of Security," *Foreign Affairs,* Spring 1993, p. 124.

Lennox, Duncan, "ATBMs and Beyond," *Jane's Defence Weekly*, May 22, 1993, p. 21.

——, "Missile Race Continues," *Jane's Defence Weekly*, January 23, 1993.

Lesser, Ian O., *Mediterranean Security: New Perspectives and Implications for U.S. Policy*, Santa Monica, CA: RAND, R-4178-AF, 1992.

——, *Security in North Africa: Internal and External Challenges*, Santa Monica, CA: RAND, MR-203-AF, 1993.

"Libya: Air Force," U.S. Naval Institute, Periscope database, June 17, 1992.

"Libya: Defense Organization/Strength," U.S. Naval Institute, Periscope database, June 17, 1992.

Lumpe, Lora, Lisbeth Gronlund, and David C. Wright, "Third World Missiles Fall Short," *Bulletin of the Atomic Scientists*, March 1992.

Lundin, S. J., "Chemical and Biological Warfare: Developments in 1988," *SIPRI Yearbook*, 1989.

McGeorge, Harvey J., "Bugs, Gas and Missiles," *Defense and Foreign Affairs*, May–June 1990.

——, "Chemical Addiction," *Defense and Foreign Affairs*, April 1989.

——, "Iraq's Secret Arsenal," *Defense and Foreign Affairs Strategic Policy*, January 1991.

——, "Reversing the Trend on Terror," *Defense and Foreign Affairs*, April 1988.

McLean, Alasdair, "European Military Space Programs," *Military Technology*, May 1992, p. 17.

Millot, Marc Dean, Roger Molander, and Peter A. Wilson, *"The Day After..." Study: Nuclear Proliferation in the Post–Cold War World*, Vol. 2 (main report), Santa Monica, CA: RAND, MR-253-AF, 1993.

Molander, Roger, "Proliferation of Weapons of Mass Destruction and Implications for Mediterranean Regional Security," in Ian Lesser and Robert Levine (eds.), *RAND/Istituto Affari Internazionali Conference on the New Mediterranean Security Environment: Conference Proceedings*, Santa Monica, CA: RAND, CF-110-RC, 1993.

Nash, Colleen, "Chemwar in the Third World," *Air Force Magazine*, January 1990.

Navias, Martin, "Is There an Emerging Third World Ballistic Missile Threat to Europe?" *RUSI Journal*, Winter 1990.

Parry, V. J., and M. E. Yapp (eds.), *War, Technology and Society in the Middle East*, London: Oxford University Press, 1975.

Perabo, Betsy, "A Chronology of Iran's Nuclear Program," *Eye on Supply*, Fall 1992, p. 64.

Porteous, Holly, "Ridding Iraq of CW to Take Two Years," *Jane's Defence Weekly*, September 28, 1991.

———, "Unravelling the Puzzle of Iraq's Nuclear Programme," *Jane's Defence Weekly*, October 5, 1991, pp. 602–603.

Rathmell, Andrew, "Chemical Weapons in the Middle East: Syria, Iran, Iraq and Libya," *Marine Corps Gazette*, July 1990.

Ripley, Tim, "Iraq's Nuclear Weapons Programme," *Jane's Intelligence Review*, December 1992.

Rubin, Uzi, "How Much Does Missile Proliferation Matter?" *Orbis*, Winter 1991.

Russian Federation Foreign Intelligence Service, "A New Challenge After the Cold War: Proliferation of Weapons of Mass Destruction," translated in JPRS-TND-93-007, 1993.

Salvy, Robert, and Jacques Clostermann, "Strength in Diversity," *International Defense Review*, January 1990.

Schaffer, Ronald, *Wings of Judgment: American Bombing in World War II*, New York: Oxford University Press, 1985.

Segal, David, "Iran Speeds Up Nuclear Bomb Development," *Journal of Defense and Diplomacy*, 1989, pp. 52–55.

Sheuy, Robert D., et al., *Missile Proliferation: Survey of Emerging Missile Forces,* Washington, D.C.: Congressional Research Service, February 9, 1989.

Smith, James, "Biological Warfare Developments," *Jane's Intelligence Review,* November 1991.

———, "Chemical Weapons Proliferation," *Jane's Soviet Intelligence Review,* May 1991.

Snyder, Jed, "Proliferation Threats to Security in NATO's Southern Region," in M. O'Brien (ed.), *Security Issues in the Mediterranean Basin,* conference proceedings, Washington, D.C.: Institute for National Strategic Studies, National Defense University, 1992.

Spector, Leonard S., and Jacqueline R. Smith, *Nuclear Ambitions: The Spread of Nuclear Weapons, 1989–1990,* Boulder: Westview Press, 1990.

Spector, Leonard S., and Nancy Blabey, "Nuclear Proliferation Threats in the Islamic Middle East," *New Outlook,* September–October 1991.

Spector, Leonard S., et al., *Tracking Nuclear Proliferation,* Washington, D.C.: Carnegie Endowment for International Peace, 1995.

"SS-1 Scud," *Jane's Strategic Weapons Systems,* Issue 10.

Stenhouse, Mark, "Cracks Along the North-South Divide," *International Defense Review,* October 1993.

"Syria and Iran Pool SRBM Resources," *Flight International,* October 22, 1991.

"Syria: Air Force," U.S. Naval Institute, Periscope database, April 28, 1992.

"Syria: Army," U.S. Naval Institute, Periscope database, April 28, 1992.

The Military Balance 1993–1994, London: IISS, 1993.

"The Year in Missiles," *Defense and Foreign Affairs,* March 1988.

U.S. Arms Control and Disarmament Agency, *Adherence to and Compliance with Arms Control Agreements and the President's Report to Congress on Soviet Noncompliance with Arms Control,* Washington, D.C.: ACDA, January 14, 1993.

U.S. Congress, Office of Technology Assessment, *Nuclear Proliferation and Safeguards,* New York: Praeger, 1977.

————, *Proliferation of Weapons of Mass Destruction: Assessing the Risks,* OTA-ISC-559, Washington, D.C.: U.S. Government Printing Office, 1993.

"Unclassified Projects: Offensive Systems," *Jane's Strategic Weapons Systems,* Issue 12.

Waters, Lee, "Chemical Weapons in the Iran/Iraq War," *Military Review,* 1990.

World Nuclear Industry Handbook 1993, Surrey, England: Nuclear Engineering International, 1993.

Wright, Claudia, "Libya's Nuclear Program," *The Middle East,* February 1982.

Wyllie, James, "Iran—Quest for Security and Influence," *Jane's Intelligence Review,* July 1993.

Zaloga, S., "Ballistic Missiles in the Third World: Scud and Beyond," *International Defense Review,* November 1988.

Zimmerman, Peter D., "Proliferation: Bronze Medal Technology Is Enough," *Orbis,* Vol. 38, No. 1, Winter 1994.